Ballym Celebration: 101 Recipes for Special Occasions

Thai Basil Bliss

Contents

INTRODUCTION

Welcome to Ballymaloe Celebration: 101 Recipes for Special Occasions - an amazing collection of recipes from Ballymaloe, one of Ireland's best known and loved cookery schools. This cookbook is packed full of delicious recipes to make any occasion unforgettable. From intimate meals to big parties, this cookbook has everything you need to make a lasting memory.

All of the recipes in this cookbook are written and prepared by the world-renowned chefs at Ballymaloe, so you can be sure to be following the recipes from some of the most well-respected culinary experts. Each recipe has been carefully tested to ensure that it is both delicious and achievable. Each recipe also features an introductory description to explain the recipe, so you can get a better understanding of what you'll be making. With plenty of illustrations to help guide you, it's easy to see just what you can make with each recipe.

Ballymaloe is renowned for its delicious and seasonal dishes, and this cookbook brings the best of them to you. With plenty of delicious starters, main courses, side dishes, desserts, and drinks, you can make a meal that will wow your friends and family every time. Whether you're throwing a dinner party, a special celebration, or just a cozy evening in, Ballymaloe has a recipe to suit.

With plenty of traditional recipes to choose from, and a few innovative dishes, you can be sure to find something to please every palate. You'll find plenty of classic recipes like Irish boxty and shepherd's pie, as well as some exciting and modern meals.

Ballymaloe Celebration: 101 Recipes for Special Occasions is the perfect cookbook to keep in your kitchen. You can be sure to find something for every occasion – quick and easy weeknight meals, celebratory feasts, or even show-stopping desserts! With the help of this cookbook, you can make sure your special occasions are even more unforgettable.

1. Roast Chicken with Herb Butter

Roast Chicken with Herb Butter is a classic and flavorful dish that is perfect for any occasion. The combination of tender chicken and aromatic herbs creates a mouthwatering meal that will impress your family and friends. This recipe is easy to follow and will result in a juicy and delicious roast chicken that is sure to be a hit.

Serving: 4 servings

Preparation time: 15 minutes

Ready time: 1 hour 30 minutes

Ingredients:
- 1 whole chicken (about 4 pounds)
- 1/2 cup unsalted butter, softened
- 2 tablespoons fresh parsley, chopped
- 2 tablespoons fresh thyme, chopped
- 2 tablespoons fresh rosemary, chopped
- 2 cloves garlic, minced
- 1 teaspoon salt
- 1/2 teaspoon black pepper

Instructions:
1. Preheat your oven to 425°F (220°C).
2. In a small bowl, combine the softened butter, chopped parsley, thyme, rosemary, minced garlic, salt, and black pepper. Mix well until all the Ingredients are evenly incorporated.
3. Carefully loosen the skin of the chicken by gently sliding your fingers between the skin and the meat. Be careful not to tear the skin.
4. Take about half of the herb butter mixture and spread it evenly under the skin of the chicken, making sure to cover as much of the meat as possible.
5. Rub the remaining herb butter mixture all over the outside of the chicken, making sure to coat it evenly.
6. Place the chicken on a roasting rack in a roasting pan, breast side up.
7. Roast the chicken in the preheated oven for about 1 hour and 15 minutes, or until the internal temperature reaches 165°F (74°C) when measured with a meat thermometer inserted into the thickest part of the thigh.

8. Once the chicken is cooked, remove it from the oven and let it rest for about 10 minutes before carving.

9. Carve the chicken into serving pieces and serve hot.

Nutrition information per Serving: - Calories: 450
- Fat: 30g
- Protein: 40g
- Carbohydrates: 1g
- Fiber: 0g
- Sugar: 0g
- Sodium: 600mg

Note: Nutrition information may vary depending on the size of the chicken and the amount of herb butter used.

2. Beef Wellington

Beef Wellington is a classic and elegant dish that is perfect for special occasions or a fancy dinner at home. This dish features tender beef fillet wrapped in a layer of savory mushroom duxelles and encased in flaky puff pastry. The result is a mouthwatering combination of flavors and textures that will impress your guests.

Serving:

This recipe serves 4 people.

Preparation time:

Preparation time for Beef Wellington is approximately 30 minutes.

Ready time:

The total cooking time for Beef Wellington is approximately 1 hour and 30 minutes.

Ingredients:
- 1 ½ pounds beef fillet
- Salt and pepper, to taste
- 2 tablespoons olive oil
- 8 ounces mushrooms, finely chopped
- 2 cloves garlic, minced
- 2 tablespoons fresh parsley, chopped
- 1 sheet puff pastry, thawed
- 1 egg, beaten (for egg wash)

Instructions:

1. Preheat your oven to 400°F (200°C).
2. Season the beef fillet with salt and pepper on all sides.
3. Heat the olive oil in a skillet over medium-high heat. Sear the beef fillet on all sides until browned. Remove from the skillet and set aside to cool.
4. In the same skillet, add the chopped mushrooms and garlic. Cook until the mushrooms release their moisture and become golden brown. Stir in the fresh parsley and season with salt and pepper to taste. Remove from heat and let it cool.
5. Roll out the puff pastry sheet on a lightly floured surface. Place the cooled mushroom mixture in the center of the pastry sheet, spreading it evenly.
6. Place the seared beef fillet on top of the mushroom mixture. Carefully wrap the puff pastry around the beef, sealing it tightly. Trim any excess pastry if needed.
7. Brush the beaten egg over the top and sides of the pastry-wrapped beef.
8. Transfer the Beef Wellington to a baking sheet lined with parchment paper. Bake in the preheated oven for about 40-45 minutes, or until the pastry is golden brown and the beef reaches your desired level of doneness.
9. Remove from the oven and let it rest for 10 minutes before slicing. Serve the Beef Wellington sliced into thick portions.

Nutrition information:

- Calories: 450 per Serving: - Fat: 25g
- Carbohydrates: 25g
- Protein: 30g
- Fiber: 2g
- Sugar: 1g
- Sodium: 350mg

Note: Nutrition information may vary depending on the specific Ingredients and brands used.

3. Seafood Paella

Seafood Paella is a classic seafood dish originating from Spain. Its colourful mix of seafood and rice makes it a very popular meal that is perfect for any dinner table.
Serving: 6 Servings
Preparation Time: 10 minutes
Ready Time: 35 minutes

Ingredients:
- 1 ½ tablespoons olive oil
- 2 cloves garlic, minced
- 1 onion, chopped
- 2 bell peppers, chopped
- 1 teaspoon smoked paprika
- 2 cups paella or bomba rice
- 3 cups fish or chicken stock
- 1 tablespoon tomato paste
- Salt and freshly ground black pepper, to taste
- 1 bay leaf
- 1 pinch saffron threads
- 1/2 pound raw shrimp, peeled and deveined
- 1 pound mussels, cleaned
- 1/2 pound calamari, cleaned and sliced

Instructions:
1. Heat the olive oil in a paella pan or a large skillet over medium-high heat. Add the garlic, onion, bell peppers and paprika and cook until the vegetables are soft, about 5 minutes.
2. Add the rice to the pan and stir to coat in the oil. Pour in the stock, tomato paste, salt and pepper, bay leaf and saffron. Stir to combine and bring to a boil, then reduce the heat to low and simmer for about 15 minutes or until the rice has absorbed the liquid and is cooked through.
3. Add the shrimp, mussels and calamari to the paella and cook for an additional 5 minutes or until the seafood is cooked through.
4. Serve the seafood paella hot.

Nutrition information: Per Serving: 230 calories, 33 g of protein, 8 g of fat, 2 g of carbohydrates, 420 mg of sodium, 2 g of fiber.

4. Irish Lamb Stew

Irish Lamb Stew is a hearty and comforting dish that is perfect for chilly evenings. This traditional Irish recipe combines tender lamb, root vegetables, and aromatic herbs to create a flavorful and satisfying stew. Whether you're celebrating St. Patrick's Day or simply craving a delicious meal, this Irish Lamb Stew is sure to impress.

Serving: 4 servings
Preparation time: 20 minutes
Ready time: 2 hours

Ingredients:
- 1.5 pounds lamb shoulder, cut into chunks
- 2 tablespoons olive oil
- 1 onion, diced
- 3 cloves garlic, minced
- 4 carrots, peeled and sliced
- 3 potatoes, peeled and diced
- 2 parsnips, peeled and sliced
- 2 tablespoons tomato paste
- 4 cups beef or vegetable broth
- 1 cup Guinness beer (optional)
- 2 bay leaves
- 1 teaspoon dried thyme
- Salt and pepper to taste
- Fresh parsley, chopped (for garnish)

Instructions:
1. Heat the olive oil in a large pot or Dutch oven over medium heat. Add the lamb chunks and brown them on all sides. Remove the lamb from the pot and set aside.
2. In the same pot, add the diced onion and minced garlic. Sauté until the onion becomes translucent and fragrant.
3. Add the tomato paste to the pot and stir well to coat the onions and garlic. Cook for an additional 2 minutes.
4. Return the lamb to the pot and add the carrots, potatoes, parsnips, bay leaves, and dried thyme. Season with salt and pepper to taste.
5. Pour in the beef or vegetable broth and Guinness beer (if using). Stir well to combine all the Ingredients.

6. Bring the stew to a boil, then reduce the heat to low. Cover the pot and simmer for about 1.5 to 2 hours, or until the lamb is tender and the flavors have melded together.
7. Remove the bay leaves from the stew before serving. Garnish with fresh parsley.
8. Serve the Irish Lamb Stew hot with crusty bread or mashed potatoes.

Nutrition information:
- Calories: 420
- Fat: 18g
- Carbohydrates: 32g
- Protein: 30g
- Fiber: 6g
- Sodium: 800mg

5. Lobster Thermidor

Lobster Thermidor is a classic French dish that showcases the rich and succulent flavors of lobster. This indulgent seafood dish is made with tender lobster meat cooked in a creamy and flavorful sauce, topped with a cheesy crust. It is a perfect choice for a special occasion or a fancy dinner party.
Serving:
This recipe serves 4 people.
Preparation time:
Preparation time for Lobster Thermidor is approximately 30 minutes.
Ready time:
The dish will be ready to serve in about 1 hour.

Ingredients:
- 2 whole lobsters (about 1 ½ pounds each)
- 4 tablespoons unsalted butter
- 1 shallot, finely chopped
- 2 cloves garlic, minced
- 1/4 cup all-purpose flour
- 1 cup whole milk
- 1/2 cup heavy cream
- 1/4 cup dry white wine

- 1/4 cup grated Gruyere cheese
- 1/4 cup grated Parmesan cheese
- 2 tablespoons Dijon mustard
- 2 tablespoons fresh parsley, chopped
- Salt and pepper to taste

Instructions:

1. Preheat your oven to 400°F (200°C).
2. Bring a large pot of salted water to a boil. Add the lobsters and cook for about 8-10 minutes until they turn bright red. Remove the lobsters from the pot and let them cool slightly.
3. Once the lobsters are cool enough to handle, crack the shells and remove the meat. Chop the lobster meat into bite-sized pieces and set aside.
4. In a large skillet, melt the butter over medium heat. Add the shallot and garlic, and sauté until they become translucent.
5. Sprinkle the flour over the shallot and garlic mixture, stirring constantly for about 1 minute to cook off the raw flour taste.
6. Slowly whisk in the milk, cream, and white wine. Continue whisking until the mixture thickens and comes to a simmer.
7. Remove the skillet from the heat and stir in the Gruyere and Parmesan cheese until melted and smooth.
8. Stir in the Dijon mustard, parsley, salt, and pepper.
9. Gently fold in the chopped lobster meat, making sure it is well coated with the sauce.
10. Transfer the lobster mixture to a baking dish and sprinkle with additional grated cheese if desired.
11. Bake in the preheated oven for about 20-25 minutes until the top is golden and bubbly.
12. Remove from the oven and let it cool for a few minutes before serving.

Nutrition information:

- Calories: 450
- Fat: 28g
- Carbohydrates: 12g
- Protein: 35g
- Fiber: 1g
- Sugar: 4g
- Sodium: 800mg

Note: The nutrition information provided is an estimate and may vary depending on the specific Ingredients used.

6. Chicken Tikka Masala

Chicken Tikka Masala is a popular Indian dish that is loved for its rich and flavorful sauce. This dish consists of tender chicken pieces marinated in a spiced yogurt mixture, grilled to perfection, and then simmered in a creamy tomato-based sauce. It is best served with steamed rice or naan bread for a complete and satisfying meal.
Serving: 4 servings
Preparation time: 20 minutes
Ready time: 1 hour 20 minutes

Ingredients:
- 1 lb (450g) boneless, skinless chicken breasts, cut into bite-sized pieces
- 1 cup plain yogurt
- 2 tablespoons lemon juice
- 2 teaspoons ground cumin
- 2 teaspoons ground paprika
- 1 teaspoon ground coriander
- 1 teaspoon ground turmeric
- 1 teaspoon ground ginger
- 1 teaspoon salt
- 1/2 teaspoon ground black pepper
- 2 tablespoons vegetable oil
- 1 large onion, finely chopped
- 4 cloves garlic, minced
- 1 tablespoon tomato paste
- 1 can (14 oz) crushed tomatoes
- 1 cup heavy cream
- 1 teaspoon garam masala
- Fresh cilantro, for garnish

Instructions:
1. In a large bowl, combine the yogurt, lemon juice, cumin, paprika, coriander, turmeric, ginger, salt, and black pepper. Mix well.

2. Add the chicken pieces to the marinade and toss until they are well coated. Cover the bowl and refrigerate for at least 1 hour, or overnight for best results.

3. Preheat your grill or broiler to medium-high heat. Thread the marinated chicken pieces onto skewers and grill or broil for about 10-12 minutes, turning occasionally, until the chicken is cooked through and slightly charred. Remove from heat and set aside.

4. In a large skillet, heat the vegetable oil over medium heat. Add the chopped onion and cook until it becomes soft and translucent, about 5 minutes. Stir in the minced garlic and cook for an additional minute.

5. Add the tomato paste to the skillet and cook for 1-2 minutes, stirring constantly. Then, add the crushed tomatoes and bring the mixture to a simmer. Cook for about 10 minutes, stirring occasionally.

6. Reduce the heat to low and stir in the heavy cream and garam masala. Simmer for an additional 5 minutes, allowing the flavors to meld together.

7. Add the grilled chicken pieces to the skillet and stir until they are well coated with the sauce. Cook for an additional 5 minutes to heat the chicken through.

8. Serve the Chicken Tikka Masala over steamed rice or with naan bread. Garnish with fresh cilantro.

Nutrition information per Serving: - Calories: 420
- Fat: 26g
- Carbohydrates: 14g
- Protein: 34g
- Fiber: 2g

7. Smoked Salmon Canapés

Smoked Salmon Canapés are elegant and delicious bite-sized appetizers that are perfect for any special occasion or gathering. These canapés feature the delicate and smoky flavor of salmon, paired with creamy and tangy Ingredients, all served on a crispy base. They are not only visually appealing but also incredibly easy to make, making them a crowd favorite.

Serving:
This recipe makes approximately 24 canapés, serving 6-8 people as an appetizer.

Preparation time:
Preparation time for these Smoked Salmon Canapés is around 15 minutes.
Ready time:
The canapés are ready to be served immediately after preparation.

Ingredients:
- 24 mini toast rounds or crackers
- 8 ounces of smoked salmon, thinly sliced
- 4 ounces of cream cheese, softened
- 2 tablespoons of fresh dill, chopped
- 1 tablespoon of lemon juice
- 1 teaspoon of capers
- Salt and pepper to taste

Instructions:
1. In a small bowl, combine the softened cream cheese, chopped dill, lemon juice, capers, salt, and pepper. Mix well until all the Ingredients are evenly incorporated.
2. Lay out the mini toast rounds or crackers on a serving platter.
3. Spread a thin layer of the cream cheese mixture onto each toast round or cracker.
4. Take a slice of smoked salmon and fold it into a small rosette shape. Place the salmon rosette on top of the cream cheese mixture on each toast round or cracker.
5. Garnish each canapé with a small sprig of fresh dill.
6. Serve immediately and enjoy!

Nutrition information:
- Serving size: 4 canapés
- Calories: 180
- Total fat: 10g
- Saturated fat: 4g
- Cholesterol: 30mg
- Sodium: 400mg
- Total carbohydrates: 14g
- Dietary fiber: 1g
- Sugars: 1g
- Protein: 9g

Note: The nutrition information provided is an estimate and may vary depending on the specific Ingredients used.

8. Rack of Lamb with Mint Sauce

Rack of Lamb with Mint Sauce is a classic dish that combines the tender and juicy flavors of lamb with the refreshing taste of mint. This elegant and flavorful dish is perfect for special occasions or a fancy dinner at home. The succulent lamb is seasoned to perfection and served with a tangy and aromatic mint sauce that complements the meat beautifully. Get ready to impress your guests with this delicious and sophisticated dish!

Serving: 4 servings
Preparation time: 15 minutes
Ready time: 45 minutes

Ingredients:
- 2 racks of lamb (about 1 ½ pounds each)
- Salt and black pepper, to taste
- 2 tablespoons olive oil
- 4 cloves of garlic, minced
- 2 tablespoons fresh rosemary, chopped
- 1 cup fresh mint leaves
- 1 tablespoon honey
- 2 tablespoons red wine vinegar
- ¼ cup extra virgin olive oil

Instructions:
1. Preheat your oven to 400°F (200°C).
2. Season the racks of lamb generously with salt and black pepper on both sides.
3. Heat the olive oil in a large oven-safe skillet over medium-high heat.
4. Sear the racks of lamb in the skillet for about 2 minutes on each side, until nicely browned.
5. Transfer the skillet to the preheated oven and roast the lamb for about 25-30 minutes for medium-rare, or until the internal temperature reaches 135°F (57°C).

6. While the lamb is roasting, prepare the mint sauce. In a blender or food processor, combine the minced garlic, chopped rosemary, mint leaves, honey, red wine vinegar, and extra virgin olive oil. Blend until smooth and well combined. Season with salt and black pepper to taste.
7. Once the lamb is cooked to your desired doneness, remove it from the oven and let it rest for about 10 minutes before slicing.
8. Slice the racks of lamb into individual chops and serve with the mint sauce on the side.
9. Enjoy your Rack of Lamb with Mint Sauce!

Nutrition information:
- Calories: 450
- Fat: 32g
- Protein: 35g
- Carbohydrates: 4g
- Fiber: 1g
- Sugar: 2g
- Sodium: 120mg

9. Coq au Vin

Coq au Vin is a classic French dish that translates to "rooster in wine." This hearty and flavorful dish is made by braising chicken in red wine, along with aromatic vegetables and herbs. The result is a tender and succulent chicken with a rich and savory sauce. Coq au Vin is a perfect dish to impress your guests or to enjoy on a cozy night in.
Serving:
This recipe serves 4 people.
Preparation time:
Preparation time for Coq au Vin is approximately 20 minutes.
Ready time:
The dish is ready to serve in about 2 hours and 30 minutes, including cooking time.

Ingredients:
- 4 chicken legs or 1 whole chicken, cut into pieces
- 4 slices of bacon, diced
- 1 onion, chopped

- 2 carrots, peeled and sliced
- 2 cloves of garlic, minced
- 8 ounces of mushrooms, sliced
- 2 cups of red wine (such as Burgundy or Pinot Noir)
- 1 cup of chicken broth
- 2 tablespoons of tomato paste
- 2 tablespoons of all-purpose flour
- 2 tablespoons of butter
- 2 sprigs of fresh thyme
- 2 bay leaves
- Salt and pepper to taste
- Chopped fresh parsley for garnish

Instructions:
1. In a large Dutch oven or heavy-bottomed pot, cook the diced bacon over medium heat until crispy. Remove the bacon from the pot and set aside, leaving the bacon fat in the pot.
2. Season the chicken pieces with salt and pepper. In the same pot with the bacon fat, brown the chicken on all sides until golden brown. Remove the chicken from the pot and set aside.
3. In the same pot, add the chopped onion, sliced carrots, minced garlic, and sliced mushrooms. Cook until the vegetables are softened, about 5 minutes.
4. Return the bacon and chicken to the pot. Add the red wine, chicken broth, tomato paste, thyme sprigs, and bay leaves. Bring the mixture to a simmer, then cover and cook over low heat for about 2 hours, or until the chicken is tender and cooked through.
5. In a small bowl, mix together the butter and flour to form a paste. Stir this paste into the pot to thicken the sauce. Cook for an additional 10 minutes, uncovered, to allow the sauce to thicken.
6. Remove the thyme sprigs and bay leaves from the pot. Taste the sauce and adjust the seasoning with salt and pepper if needed.
7. Serve the Coq au Vin hot, garnished with chopped fresh parsley. It pairs well with crusty bread or mashed potatoes.

Nutrition information:
(Note: Nutrition information may vary depending on the specific Ingredients used and serving size.)

- Calories: Approximately 450 per Serving: - Fat: Approximately 25g per Serving: - Carbohydrates: Approximately 10g per Serving: - Protein: Approximately 35g per serving

10. Baked Salmon with Dill Sauce

Baked Salmon with Dill Sauce is a delicious and healthy dish that is perfect for any occasion. The combination of tender salmon fillets and creamy dill sauce creates a mouthwatering flavor that will leave you wanting more. This recipe is easy to make and is sure to impress your family and friends.
Serving: 4 servings
Preparation time: 10 minutes
Ready time: 30 minutes

Ingredients:
- 4 salmon fillets (about 6 ounces each)
- Salt and pepper to taste
- 2 tablespoons olive oil
- 1 tablespoon fresh dill, chopped
- 1 tablespoon fresh lemon juice
- 1 cup Greek yogurt
- 2 tablespoons mayonnaise
- 1 tablespoon Dijon mustard
- 1 clove garlic, minced

Instructions:
1. Preheat the oven to 400°F (200°C). Line a baking sheet with parchment paper.
2. Season the salmon fillets with salt and pepper on both sides.
3. In a small bowl, combine the olive oil, chopped dill, and lemon juice. Brush the mixture over the salmon fillets.
4. Place the salmon fillets on the prepared baking sheet and bake for 15-20 minutes, or until the salmon is cooked through and flakes easily with a fork.
5. While the salmon is baking, prepare the dill sauce. In a medium bowl, whisk together the Greek yogurt, mayonnaise, Dijon mustard, and minced garlic until well combined.

6. Serve the baked salmon with the dill sauce on the side or drizzled over the top. Garnish with additional fresh dill, if desired.

Nutrition information:
- Calories: 350
- Fat: 20g
- Protein: 35g
- Carbohydrates: 5g
- Fiber: 1g
- Sugar: 3g
- Sodium: 300mg

Note: Nutrition information may vary depending on the specific Ingredients and brands used.

11. Beef Bourguignon

Beef Bourguignon is a classic French dish that is rich, flavorful, and perfect for a cozy dinner. This dish features tender beef cooked in a red wine sauce, along with aromatic vegetables and herbs. It is a hearty and comforting meal that is sure to impress your family and friends.

Serving: 4 servings
Preparation time: 20 minutes
Ready time: 2 hours 30 minutes

Ingredients:
- 2 pounds beef chuck, cut into 1-inch cubes
- 4 slices bacon, chopped
- 1 onion, diced
- 2 carrots, sliced
- 2 cloves garlic, minced
- 1 cup red wine (such as Burgundy or Pinot Noir)
- 2 cups beef broth
- 2 tablespoons tomato paste
- 1 tablespoon all-purpose flour
- 1 tablespoon olive oil
- 1 bay leaf
- 1 teaspoon dried thyme
- Salt and pepper, to taste

- Fresh parsley, for garnish

Instructions:
1. In a large Dutch oven or heavy-bottomed pot, cook the bacon over medium heat until crispy. Remove the bacon and set aside, leaving the rendered fat in the pot.
2. Season the beef cubes with salt and pepper. In the same pot with the bacon fat, brown the beef in batches over medium-high heat until well-browned on all sides. Remove the beef and set aside.
3. In the same pot, add the diced onion, sliced carrots, and minced garlic. Cook for about 5 minutes, or until the vegetables are softened.
4. Add the tomato paste and flour to the pot, stirring well to coat the vegetables. Cook for an additional 2 minutes.
5. Slowly pour in the red wine, scraping the bottom of the pot to release any browned bits. Bring the mixture to a simmer and cook for 5 minutes, allowing the wine to reduce slightly.
6. Return the beef and bacon to the pot, along with the beef broth, bay leaf, and dried thyme. Stir well to combine.
7. Cover the pot and simmer over low heat for 2 hours, or until the beef is tender and the flavors have melded together.
8. Remove the bay leaf and season with additional salt and pepper, if needed.
9. Serve the Beef Bourguignon hot, garnished with fresh parsley. It pairs well with mashed potatoes, rice, or crusty bread.

Nutrition information per Serving: - Calories: 450
- Fat: 20g
- Carbohydrates: 10g
- Protein: 50g
- Fiber: 2g

12. Irish Soda Bread

Irish Soda Bread is a traditional quick bread from Ireland that is made with just basic pantry staples. This light, fluffy and slightly sweet bread tastes best when served warm with butter.
Serving: Makes 12 servings
Preparation Time: 10 minutes

Ready Time: 40 minutes

Ingredients:
-2 cups all-purpose flour
-1 teaspoon baking soda
-1 teaspoon fine sea salt
-3 tablespoons sugar
-1/4 cup (1/2 stick) salted or unsalted butter, chilled and cut into cubes
-3/4 cup plain yogurt
-1/4 cup buttermilk
-1 large egg, beaten

Instructions:
1. Preheat oven to 350°F and coat a baking sheet with cooking spray or line with parchment paper.
2. In a large bowl, whisk together the flour, baking soda, salt, and sugar.
3. Use a pastry cutter or your hands to mix in the butter until it's evenly incorporated into the dry Ingredients.
4. In a separate bowl, whisk together the yogurt, buttermilk, and egg.
5. Pour the wet Ingredients into the dry Ingredients and mix until everything is combined.
6. Form the dough into a ball and place it onto the prepared baking sheet. Score the top of the dough with a shallow X and bake for 40 minutes, or until the top is golden brown.
7. Let cool before slicing and serving.

Nutrition information: Calories: 194, Fat: 7g, Saturated Fat: 4g, Cholesterol: 34mg, Sodium: 247mg, Carbohydrates: 27g, Fiber: 1g, Sugar: 4g, Protein: 5g.

13. Chicken Parmesan

Chicken Parmesan is a classic Italian dish that combines tender chicken breasts with a flavorful tomato sauce and melted cheese. This dish is perfect for a family dinner or a special occasion. The crispy breaded chicken, tangy tomato sauce, and gooey cheese make for a delicious and satisfying meal.
Serving: 4 servings

Preparation time: 15 minutes
Ready time: 45 minutes

Ingredients:
- 4 boneless, skinless chicken breasts
- 1 cup breadcrumbs
- 1/2 cup grated Parmesan cheese
- 1 teaspoon dried oregano
- 1 teaspoon dried basil
- 1/2 teaspoon garlic powder
- Salt and pepper to taste
- 2 eggs, beaten
- 1 cup marinara sauce
- 1 cup shredded mozzarella cheese
- Fresh basil leaves for garnish (optional)

Instructions:
1. Preheat the oven to 375°F (190°C). Grease a baking dish with cooking spray or olive oil.
2. In a shallow dish, combine the breadcrumbs, grated Parmesan cheese, dried oregano, dried basil, garlic powder, salt, and pepper.
3. Dip each chicken breast into the beaten eggs, then coat it with the breadcrumb mixture, pressing gently to adhere the breadcrumbs to the chicken.
4. Place the breaded chicken breasts in the greased baking dish and bake for 25 minutes, or until the chicken is cooked through and the breadcrumbs are golden brown.
5. Remove the baking dish from the oven and spoon marinara sauce over each chicken breast. Sprinkle shredded mozzarella cheese on top.
6. Return the baking dish to the oven and bake for an additional 10 minutes, or until the cheese is melted and bubbly.
7. Remove from the oven and let the chicken rest for a few minutes before serving. Garnish with fresh basil leaves, if desired.
8. Serve the Chicken Parmesan hot with a side of pasta or a green salad.

Nutrition information per Serving: - Calories: 380
- Fat: 14g
- Carbohydrates: 20g
- Protein: 42g
- Fiber: 2g

- Sugar: 4g
- Sodium: 800mg

Note: Nutrition information may vary depending on the specific Ingredients and brands used.

14. Seafood Chowder

Seafood Chowder is a hearty and flavorful dish that combines the goodness of various seafood with a creamy and rich broth. This comforting soup is perfect for chilly evenings or as a special treat for seafood lovers. Packed with protein and essential nutrients, this Seafood Chowder is a complete meal in itself.

Serving:

This recipe serves 4 people.

Preparation time:

Preparation time for this Seafood Chowder is approximately 20 minutes.

Ready time:

The Seafood Chowder will be ready to serve in about 40 minutes.

Ingredients:
- 1 tablespoon butter
- 1 onion, diced
- 2 cloves of garlic, minced
- 2 medium potatoes, peeled and diced
- 2 cups fish or seafood stock
- 1 cup milk
- 1 cup heavy cream
- 1 bay leaf
- 1 teaspoon dried thyme
- 1/2 teaspoon paprika
- Salt and pepper to taste
- 1 cup mixed seafood (such as shrimp, scallops, and fish), diced
- Fresh parsley, chopped (for garnish)

Instructions:
1. In a large pot, melt the butter over medium heat. Add the diced onion and minced garlic, and sauté until they become translucent and fragrant.

2. Add the diced potatoes to the pot and stir well to coat them with the butter and onion mixture.

3. Pour in the fish or seafood stock, milk, and heavy cream. Stir in the bay leaf, dried thyme, paprika, salt, and pepper. Bring the mixture to a simmer and let it cook for about 15-20 minutes, or until the potatoes are tender.

4. Once the potatoes are cooked, add the mixed seafood to the pot. Cook for an additional 5-7 minutes, or until the seafood is cooked through and opaque.

5. Remove the bay leaf from the pot and discard it. Taste the chowder and adjust the seasoning if needed.

6. Ladle the Seafood Chowder into bowls and garnish with fresh parsley.

7. Serve hot and enjoy!

Nutrition information:
- Calories: 350 per Serving: - Total fat: 20g
- Cholesterol: 100mg
- Sodium: 500mg
- Total carbohydrates: 25g
- Protein: 18g
Note: The nutrition information provided is an estimate and may vary depending on the specific Ingredients used.

15. Beef and Guinness Pie

Beef and Guinness Pie is a hearty and flavorful dish that combines tender beef, rich Guinness beer, and a buttery pastry crust. This traditional Irish recipe is perfect for a cozy dinner on a cold evening or for celebrating St. Patrick's Day. The slow-cooked beef and Guinness filling is packed with savory flavors that will leave you wanting more.
Serving: 4 servings
Preparation time: 30 minutes
Ready time: 3 hours 30 minutes

Ingredients:
- 1.5 pounds (700g) beef stew meat, cut into bite-sized pieces
- 1 tablespoon vegetable oil
- 1 large onion, diced

- 2 cloves of garlic, minced
- 2 carrots, peeled and diced
- 2 celery stalks, diced
- 1 cup Guinness beer
- 1 cup beef broth
- 2 tablespoons tomato paste
- 1 tablespoon Worcestershire sauce
- 1 teaspoon dried thyme
- Salt and pepper to taste
- 2 tablespoons all-purpose flour
- 1 sheet of puff pastry, thawed
- 1 egg, beaten (for egg wash)

Instructions:
1. Preheat your oven to 325°F (160°C).
2. In a large oven-safe pot or Dutch oven, heat the vegetable oil over medium-high heat. Add the beef stew meat and brown it on all sides. Remove the beef from the pot and set it aside.
3. In the same pot, add the diced onion, minced garlic, carrots, and celery. Sauté until the vegetables are softened, about 5 minutes.
4. Return the beef to the pot and pour in the Guinness beer and beef broth. Stir in the tomato paste, Worcestershire sauce, dried thyme, salt, and pepper. Bring the mixture to a simmer.
5. Cover the pot with a lid and transfer it to the preheated oven. Allow the beef and Guinness mixture to cook for 2.5 to 3 hours, or until the beef is tender and the flavors have melded together.
6. Once the beef is cooked, remove the pot from the oven and place it back on the stovetop over medium heat. Sprinkle the flour over the mixture and stir well to thicken the sauce. Cook for an additional 5 minutes until the sauce has thickened.
7. Increase the oven temperature to 400°F (200°C). Transfer the beef and Guinness filling to a pie dish or individual ramekins.
8. Roll out the puff pastry sheet on a lightly floured surface. Cut it into a shape that will fit over the pie dish or ramekins. Place the pastry over the filling, pressing the edges to seal. Cut a few slits on the top to allow steam to escape.
9. Brush the beaten egg over the pastry to create a golden crust. Place the pie dish or ramekins on a baking sheet and bake in the preheated oven for 20-25 minutes, or until the pastry is puffed and golden.

10. Remove from the oven and let it cool for a few minutes before serving. Enjoy the Beef and Guinness Pie while it's still warm.

Nutrition information per Serving: - Calories: 450
- Fat: 22g
- Carbohydrates: 28g
- Protein: 32g
- Fiber: 3g

16. Roast Pork with Apple Sauce

Roast Pork with Apple Sauce is a classic comforting meal that's perfect for any occasion. This tasty dish features pork shoulder or loin roasted to perfection and served with homemade apple sauce for a delicious flavor combination.
Serving: 6
Preparation Time: 15 minutes
Ready Time: 1 hour 15 minutes

Ingredients:
- 1 pork shoulder or loin (about 2 to 2.5lbs/1kg)
- 2 tablespoons olive or vegetable oil
- Salt and freshly ground pepper
- 2 apples, peeled, cored and sliced
- 2 tablespoons white wine vinegar
- 2 tablespoons apple juice
- 2 tablespoons light brown sugar

Instructions:
1. Preheat oven to 425°F (220°C).
2. Rub the pork with the oil and season with salt and pepper.
3. Place on a baking sheet and roast for about 1 hour, until cooked through.
4. Meanwhile, place the apples, sugar, vinegar and juice in a saucepan. Simmer over low heat for 10 minutes until the apples are soft.
5. Once cooked, remove the pork from the oven and allow to rest for 10 minutes before slicing. Serve with the apple sauce.

Nutrition information: Per serving (excluding unknown items): 282 Calories; 17.8g Fat (55.6% calories from fat); 28g Protein; 6.7g Carbohydrate; 1.3g Dietary Fiber; 71mg Cholesterol; 264mg Sodium.

17. Grilled Shrimp Skewers

Grilled shrimp skewers are a delicious way to enjoy succulent, flavorful, juicy grilled shrimp in no time at all. Serve them alone as a light meal or appetizer or stack them on top of a salad or pasta for a complete flavorful meal.
Serving: 4
Preparation Time: 10 minutes
Ready Time: 10 minutes

Ingredients:
• 1 lb. shrimp, peeled and deveined
• 2 tablespoons olive oil
• 2 tablespoons fresh lemon juice
• 1 teaspoon garlic powder
• Salt and pepper, to taste
• 8 metal or wooden skewers

Instructions:
1. Preheat the grill over medium heat.
2. In a large bowl, mix together the shrimp, olive oil, lemon juice, garlic powder, and salt and pepper. Gently stir until the shrimp are evenly coated.
3. Place the shrimp on the skewers, leaving a little room between the shrimp.
4. Place the shrimp skewers on the preheated grill. Cook for 5 minutes, then flip and cook for an additional 4-5 minutes until the shrimp is cooked through.
5. Remove from the grill and serve with desired accompaniments.

Nutrition information:
Serving size: 4 servings
Calories: 203

Total Fat: 8g
Saturated Fat: 1.2g
Cholesterol: 192.3mg
Sodium: 381.5mg
Carbohydrates: 2.3g
Fiber: 0.2g
Sugar: 0.3g
Protein: 28.4g

18. Shepherd's Pie

Shepherd's Pie is a classic comfort food dish that originated in the United Kingdom. It is a hearty and delicious meal that combines ground meat, vegetables, and mashed potatoes. This dish is perfect for a cozy family dinner or for entertaining guests. With its rich flavors and creamy texture, Shepherd's Pie is sure to become a favorite in your household.
Serving:
This recipe serves 6 people.
Preparation time:
Preparation time for Shepherd's Pie is approximately 30 minutes.
Ready time:
The total cooking time for Shepherd's Pie is approximately 1 hour and 15 minutes.

Ingredients:
- 1 ½ pounds ground beef or lamb
- 1 onion, finely chopped
- 2 carrots, diced
- 2 cloves of garlic, minced
- 1 cup frozen peas
- 2 tablespoons tomato paste
- 1 cup beef or vegetable broth
- 1 teaspoon Worcestershire sauce
- 1 teaspoon dried thyme
- Salt and pepper to taste
- 4 cups mashed potatoes
- 1 cup shredded cheddar cheese

Instructions:

1. Preheat your oven to 375°F (190°C).
2. In a large skillet, cook the ground beef or lamb over medium heat until browned. Drain any excess fat.
3. Add the chopped onion, diced carrots, and minced garlic to the skillet. Cook for 5 minutes, or until the vegetables have softened.
4. Stir in the frozen peas, tomato paste, beef or vegetable broth, Worcestershire sauce, dried thyme, salt, and pepper. Simmer for 10 minutes, allowing the flavors to meld together.
5. Transfer the meat mixture to a 9x13-inch baking dish and spread it evenly.
6. Spread the mashed potatoes over the meat mixture, ensuring it covers the entire surface.
7. Sprinkle the shredded cheddar cheese on top of the mashed potatoes.
8. Bake in the preheated oven for 30-35 minutes, or until the cheese is melted and bubbly.
9. Allow the Shepherd's Pie to cool for a few minutes before serving.

Nutrition information:

- Calories: 450
- Fat: 20g
- Carbohydrates: 35g
- Protein: 30g
- Fiber: 5g

Note: The nutrition information provided is an estimate and may vary depending on the specific Ingredients used.

19. Seafood Risotto

Seafood Risotto is a delicious and creamy Italian dish that combines the flavors of fresh seafood with the richness of Arborio rice. This dish is perfect for seafood lovers and makes for a satisfying and comforting meal. With a few simple Ingredients and some patience, you can create a restaurant-quality seafood risotto right in your own kitchen.

Serving: 4 servings
Preparation time: 10 minutes
Ready time: 40 minutes

Ingredients:
- 1 cup Arborio rice
- 1/2 cup white wine
- 4 cups seafood or vegetable broth
- 1/2 onion, finely chopped
- 2 cloves garlic, minced
- 1/2 cup grated Parmesan cheese
- 1/4 cup heavy cream
- 1/2 pound mixed seafood (such as shrimp, scallops, and mussels)
- 2 tablespoons olive oil
- Salt and pepper to taste
- Fresh parsley, chopped (for garnish)

Instructions:
1. In a large saucepan, heat the olive oil over medium heat. Add the chopped onion and minced garlic, and sauté until they become translucent and fragrant.
2. Add the Arborio rice to the saucepan and stir it around for a minute or two, allowing it to toast slightly. This will help give the risotto a nutty flavor.
3. Pour in the white wine and stir until it is absorbed by the rice. This step will add a subtle acidity to the dish.
4. Begin adding the seafood or vegetable broth, one ladleful at a time, stirring constantly. Allow each ladleful to be absorbed by the rice before adding the next. This slow and gradual process is what gives risotto its creamy texture.
5. While the risotto is cooking, prepare the mixed seafood. If using shrimp, peel and devein them. If using scallops, remove the muscle on the side. Clean the mussels and discard any that are open or broken.
6. In a separate pan, heat a tablespoon of olive oil over medium-high heat. Add the seafood and cook until they are just cooked through. Be careful not to overcook them, as they can become tough and rubbery.
7. Once the risotto is cooked and creamy, stir in the grated Parmesan cheese and heavy cream. Season with salt and pepper to taste.
8. Gently fold in the cooked seafood, being careful not to break them apart. Allow the risotto to rest for a few minutes to let the flavors meld together.
9. Serve the seafood risotto hot, garnished with freshly chopped parsley. Enjoy!

Nutrition information:
- Calories: 450
- Fat: 15g
- Carbohydrates: 55g
- Protein: 20g
- Fiber: 2g

20. Corned Beef and Cabbage

Corned Beef and Cabbage is an Irish dish that is a popular traditional source of nourishment and comfort. It features corned beef which is primarily boiled with chunks of carrots and cabbage.
Serving: 4
Preparation time: 10 minutes
Ready Time: 75 minutes

Ingredients:
1 corned beef brisket, four to five pounds
2-3 garlic cloves, minced
2 quarts of water
4 carrots – peeled and diced
1 cabbage – chopped into small wedges
2 bay leaves
2 crushed juniper berries

Instructions:
1. Place the corned beef brisket into a large pot and fill it with two quarts of water.
2. Add garlic, carrots, cabbage, bay leaves and crushed juniper berries to the pot.
3. Bring the mixture to a boil and cover the pot. Turn down the heat and allow the mixture to simmer for up to one and a half hours, until the corned beef is tender.
4. Once the meat has cooked, use a slotted spoon to remove it from the liquid. Slice the meat against the grain to get the most tender pieces.
5. Finally, place the remaining vegetables into a serving dish and top with the sliced corned beef.

Nutrition information:
Serving size: 4 ounces of corned beef
Calories: 230
Total fat: 12 g
Carbohydrates: 5 g
Protein: 25 g

21. Chicken Piccata

Chicken Piccata is a classic Italian dish that features tender chicken breasts cooked in a tangy and flavorful lemon-caper sauce. This dish is perfect for a quick and delicious weeknight dinner or for impressing guests at a dinner party. The combination of the bright citrus flavors and the briny capers creates a mouthwatering dish that is sure to please everyone at the table.
Serving: 4 servings
Preparation time: 10 minutes
Ready time: 25 minutes

Ingredients:
- 4 boneless, skinless chicken breasts
- Salt and pepper, to taste
- 1/2 cup all-purpose flour
- 2 tablespoons olive oil
- 4 tablespoons unsalted butter
- 1/2 cup chicken broth
- 1/4 cup fresh lemon juice
- 1/4 cup brined capers, drained
- 2 tablespoons chopped fresh parsley, for garnish

Instructions:
1. Start by pounding the chicken breasts to an even thickness of about 1/4 inch. Season both sides of the chicken breasts with salt and pepper.
2. Place the flour in a shallow dish and dredge each chicken breast in the flour, shaking off any excess.
3. In a large skillet, heat the olive oil and 2 tablespoons of butter over medium-high heat. Once the butter has melted and the skillet is hot, add the chicken breasts to the skillet. Cook for about 3-4 minutes on each

side, or until golden brown and cooked through. Remove the chicken from the skillet and set aside.

4. In the same skillet, add the chicken broth, lemon juice, and capers. Bring the mixture to a boil and let it simmer for about 2 minutes, or until slightly reduced.

5. Remove the skillet from the heat and stir in the remaining 2 tablespoons of butter until melted and incorporated into the sauce.

6. Place the chicken breasts back into the skillet, spooning the sauce over the top. Garnish with chopped parsley.

7. Serve the Chicken Piccata hot with your choice of side dishes, such as pasta or roasted vegetables.

Nutrition information per Serving: - Calories: 350
- Fat: 18g
- Carbohydrates: 12g
- Protein: 34g
- Fiber: 1g
- Sugar: 1g
- Sodium: 450mg

22. Bouillabaisse

Bouillabaisse is a traditional French seafood stew that originated in the port city of Marseille. This flavorful dish is a true celebration of the sea, combining a variety of fresh fish and shellfish with aromatic herbs and spices. Bouillabaisse is not only delicious but also a great way to showcase the bounty of the ocean. So, let's dive into this classic recipe and bring a taste of the Mediterranean to your table!

Serving: 4 servings
Preparation time: 30 minutes
Ready time: 1 hour 30 minutes

Ingredients:
- 1 lb (450g) mixed fish fillets (such as cod, halibut, or sea bass), cut into chunks
- 1 lb (450g) mixed shellfish (such as mussels, clams, and shrimp), cleaned and debearded
- 1 onion, finely chopped

- 2 cloves of garlic, minced
- 1 fennel bulb, thinly sliced
- 1 red bell pepper, diced
- 1 can (14 oz/400g) diced tomatoes
- 2 tablespoons tomato paste
- 2 cups fish or vegetable broth
- 1 cup dry white wine
- 2 tablespoons olive oil
- 1 teaspoon saffron threads
- 1 bay leaf
- 1 teaspoon dried thyme
- Salt and pepper to taste
- Fresh parsley, chopped (for garnish)
- Crusty bread (for serving)

Instructions:

1. In a large pot or Dutch oven, heat the olive oil over medium heat. Add the chopped onion, minced garlic, sliced fennel, and diced red bell pepper. Sauté for about 5 minutes until the vegetables are softened.
2. Stir in the tomato paste and cook for another minute. Then add the diced tomatoes, fish or vegetable broth, white wine, saffron threads, bay leaf, and dried thyme. Season with salt and pepper to taste. Bring the mixture to a simmer and let it cook for about 30 minutes to allow the flavors to meld together.
3. After the broth has simmered, add the fish chunks to the pot and cook for about 5 minutes until they are just cooked through. Then add the shellfish, cover the pot, and cook for an additional 5 minutes until the shells have opened and the shrimp are pink and opaque.
4. Remove the bay leaf from the pot and taste the broth for seasoning. Adjust with salt and pepper if needed. Ladle the bouillabaisse into bowls, garnish with fresh parsley, and serve with crusty bread on the side.

Nutrition information:

- Calories: 350 per Serving: - Fat: 10g
- Carbohydrates: 20g
- Protein: 40g
- Fiber: 4g
- Sodium: 800mg

Note: The nutrition information provided is an estimate and may vary depending on the specific Ingredients used.

23. Stuffed Bell Peppers

Stuffed Bell Peppers are a delicious and nutritious dish that combines the vibrant flavors of bell peppers with a savory filling. This recipe is perfect for a hearty and satisfying meal that can be enjoyed by the whole family.
Serving: 4 servings
Preparation time: 20 minutes
Ready time: 1 hour

Ingredients:
- 4 large bell peppers (any color)
- 1 pound ground beef
- 1 cup cooked rice
- 1 small onion, diced
- 2 cloves garlic, minced
- 1 cup tomato sauce
- 1 teaspoon dried oregano
- 1 teaspoon dried basil
- Salt and pepper to taste
- 1 cup shredded mozzarella cheese

Instructions:
1. Preheat your oven to 375°F (190°C).
2. Cut the tops off the bell peppers and remove the seeds and membranes. Rinse the peppers under cold water and set aside.
3. In a large skillet, cook the ground beef over medium heat until browned. Drain any excess fat.
4. Add the diced onion and minced garlic to the skillet with the ground beef. Cook for an additional 2-3 minutes until the onion is translucent.
5. Stir in the cooked rice, tomato sauce, dried oregano, dried basil, salt, and pepper. Cook for another 5 minutes, allowing the flavors to meld together.
6. Place the bell peppers in a baking dish and fill each pepper with the ground beef mixture. Top each pepper with a generous amount of shredded mozzarella cheese.
7. Cover the baking dish with aluminum foil and bake in the preheated oven for 45 minutes.

8. After 45 minutes, remove the foil and continue baking for an additional 10-15 minutes until the cheese is golden and bubbly.
9. Remove from the oven and let the stuffed bell peppers cool for a few minutes before serving.

Nutrition information per Serving: - Calories: 350
- Fat: 15g
- Carbohydrates: 25g
- Protein: 25g
- Fiber: 4g

24. Baked Ham with Honey Glaze

Baked Ham with Honey Glaze is a classic dish that is perfect for special occasions or holiday gatherings. The combination of the tender ham and the sweet and sticky honey glaze creates a mouthwatering flavor that will leave your guests wanting more. This recipe is easy to follow and will surely impress your family and friends.
Serving: 8-10 servings
Preparation time: 15 minutes
Ready time: 2 hours 30 minutes

Ingredients:
- 1 (8-10 pounds) fully cooked bone-in ham
- 1 cup honey
- 1/2 cup brown sugar
- 1/4 cup Dijon mustard
- 2 tablespoons apple cider vinegar
- 1 teaspoon ground cinnamon
- 1/2 teaspoon ground cloves

Instructions:
1. Preheat your oven to 325°F (165°C).
2. Place the ham in a large roasting pan, fat side up. Score the surface of the ham in a diamond pattern with a sharp knife, making sure not to cut too deep.
3. In a small saucepan, combine the honey, brown sugar, Dijon mustard, apple cider vinegar, ground cinnamon, and ground cloves. Cook over

medium heat, stirring constantly, until the mixture is smooth and well combined.

4. Pour half of the honey glaze over the ham, making sure to brush it evenly over the surface. Reserve the remaining glaze for later.

5. Cover the ham loosely with aluminum foil and bake for about 2 hours, or until the internal temperature reaches 140°F (60°C). Baste the ham with the pan juices every 30 minutes.

6. Remove the foil and brush the remaining honey glaze over the ham. Increase the oven temperature to 375°F (190°C) and bake for an additional 30 minutes, or until the glaze is caramelized and the ham is golden brown.

7. Remove the ham from the oven and let it rest for about 15 minutes before slicing. Serve warm and enjoy!

Nutrition information:
- Calories: 350 per Serving: - Total fat: 12g
- Cholesterol: 80mg
- Sodium: 1200mg
- Total carbohydrates: 35g
- Protein: 25g

Note: Nutrition information may vary depending on the specific brand of Ingredients used.

25. Fish and Chips

Fish and chips is a classic British dish that has gained popularity all over the world. This delicious meal consists of crispy battered fish served with golden fries. It is a perfect combination of flavors and textures that will satisfy your cravings for a hearty and comforting meal. Whether you're hosting a casual gathering or simply want to indulge in a tasty treat, fish and chips is always a great choice.

Serving: 4 servings
Preparation time: 15 minutes
Ready time: 30 minutes

Ingredients:
- 4 white fish fillets (such as cod or haddock)
- 1 cup all-purpose flour

- 1 teaspoon baking powder
- 1 teaspoon salt
- 1/2 teaspoon black pepper
- 1 cup cold sparkling water
- Vegetable oil, for frying
- 4 large potatoes, cut into fries
- Salt, to taste
- Malt vinegar, for Serving: - Tartar sauce, for Serving:

Instructions:
1. In a large bowl, whisk together the flour, baking powder, salt, and black pepper. Gradually add the sparkling water while whisking until a smooth batter forms. Set aside.
2. Heat vegetable oil in a deep fryer or large pot to 375°F (190°C).
3. Pat the fish fillets dry with paper towels and season with salt and pepper.
4. Dip each fish fillet into the batter, allowing any excess to drip off, then carefully place it into the hot oil. Fry the fish for about 4-5 minutes on each side, or until golden brown and crispy. Remove from the oil and drain on a paper towel-lined plate.
5. In the same oil, fry the potato fries in batches until golden and crispy. Remove from the oil and drain on a paper towel-lined plate. Sprinkle with salt while still hot.
6. Serve the fish and chips hot with malt vinegar and tartar sauce on the side.

Nutrition information per Serving: - Calories: 450
- Fat: 15g
- Carbohydrates: 55g
- Protein: 25g
- Fiber: 4g
Note: Nutrition information may vary depending on the type and amount of fish used, as well as the cooking method for the fries.

26. Chicken Alfredo

Chicken Alfredo is a creamy and delicious Italian-American pasta dish. This easy-to-make recipe will become one of your favorite go-to dinners that you can make for the family.

Serving: 4
Preparation time: 10 minutes
Ready time: 30 minutes

Ingredients:

- 2 tablespoons olive oil
- 2 tablespoons butter
- 2 cloves fresh garlic, minced
- 2 cups chicken broth
- 2 cups heavy cream
- 1 ½ cups grated Parmesan cheese (or vegan alternative such as Nutritional Yeast)
- 1 teaspoon pepper
- ¼ teaspoon sea salt
- 8 ounces uncooked penne pasta
- 2 cups shredded cooked chicken

Instructions:

1. Heat olive oil and butter in a large saucepan on medium-high heat.
2. Add garlic and cook until fragrant, about 1 minute.
3. Pour in chicken broth and heavy cream, and whisk to combine.
4. Add Parmesan cheese, pepper, and salt, and stir until cheese is melted and sauce is smooth.
5. Turn heat to low and simmer for 15 minutes, stirring occasionally.
6. While sauce is cooking, bring a large pot of salted water to a boil and add penne. Cook for 10-12 minutes, or according to package directions, until pasta is al dente.
7. Drain pasta and add to sauce pan with sauce.
8. Add chicken and stir until heated through.
9. Serve warm with extra Parmesan cheese or vegan alternative.

Nutrition information: per serving: Calories 533, Fat 35 g, Cholesterol 140 g, Sodium 1000 mg, Carbohydrate 26 g, Protein 27 g.

27. Irish Boxty

Irish Boxty is a traditional Irish dish that combines the flavors of a potato pancake and a traditional Irish potato cake. It is a hearty and delicious dish that is perfect for breakfast or as a side dish for any meal. The Boxty is made with grated potatoes, flour, and buttermilk, resulting in a crispy and flavorful pancake that is sure to please your taste buds.
Serving: 4 servings
Preparation time: 15 minutes
Ready time: 30 minutes

Ingredients:
- 2 large potatoes, peeled and grated
- 1 cup all-purpose flour
- 1 teaspoon baking powder
- 1/2 teaspoon salt
- 1/4 teaspoon black pepper
- 1/2 cup buttermilk
- 2 tablespoons butter, melted
- 1 tablespoon vegetable oil

Instructions:
1. In a large bowl, combine the grated potatoes, flour, baking powder, salt, and black pepper. Mix well to ensure all the Ingredients are evenly distributed.
2. Add the buttermilk and melted butter to the potato mixture. Stir until everything is well combined and a thick batter forms.
3. Heat the vegetable oil in a large skillet over medium heat.
4. Drop spoonfuls of the potato batter onto the hot skillet, spreading them out to form pancakes about 4 inches in diameter. Cook for about 3-4 minutes on each side, or until golden brown and crispy.
5. Remove the Boxty from the skillet and place them on a paper towel-lined plate to drain any excess oil.
6. Serve the Irish Boxty hot with your favorite toppings, such as sour cream, chives, or smoked salmon.

Nutrition information per Serving: - Calories: 250
- Fat: 8g
- Carbohydrates: 38g
- Protein: 6g

- Fiber: 3g
Note: Nutrition information may vary depending on the specific
Ingredients and brands used.

28. Beef Stroganoff

Beef Stroganoff is a classic Russian dish that has gained popularity
worldwide. This hearty and flavorful dish features tender strips of beef
cooked in a creamy sauce, served over a bed of egg noodles or rice. It is
the perfect comfort food for a cozy dinner at home or for entertaining
guests.
Serving: 4 servings
Preparation time: 15 minutes
Ready time: 30 minutes

Ingredients:
- 1 pound beef sirloin, cut into thin strips
- 1 onion, thinly sliced
- 2 cloves garlic, minced
- 8 ounces mushrooms, sliced
- 2 tablespoons butter
- 1 tablespoon olive oil
- 1 cup beef broth
- 1 cup sour cream
- 2 tablespoons all-purpose flour
- 1 tablespoon Dijon mustard
- Salt and pepper to taste
- Fresh parsley, chopped (for garnish)
- Egg noodles or rice (for serving)

Instructions:
1. In a large skillet, heat the butter and olive oil over medium-high heat.
Add the beef strips and cook until browned on all sides. Remove the
beef from the skillet and set aside.
2. In the same skillet, add the sliced onion and minced garlic. Sauté until
the onion becomes translucent and fragrant.
3. Add the sliced mushrooms to the skillet and cook until they release
their moisture and start to brown.

4. In a small bowl, whisk together the beef broth, sour cream, flour, and Dijon mustard until well combined.

5. Pour the sour cream mixture into the skillet with the onions and mushrooms. Stir well to combine.

6. Return the beef strips to the skillet and simmer for about 10 minutes, or until the sauce thickens and the beef is cooked to your desired level of doneness.

7. Season with salt and pepper to taste.

8. Serve the beef stroganoff over a bed of cooked egg noodles or rice.

9. Garnish with fresh chopped parsley.

Nutrition information:
- Calories: 420
- Fat: 25g
- Carbohydrates: 15g
- Protein: 35g
- Fiber: 2g
- Sugar: 4g
- Sodium: 450mg

Note: Nutrition information may vary depending on the specific Ingredients and brands used.

29. Scallops with Garlic Butter

Scallops with Garlic Butter is a delicious and elegant seafood dish that is perfect for a special occasion or a fancy dinner at home. The succulent scallops are cooked to perfection and then coated in a rich and flavorful garlic butter sauce. This dish is sure to impress your guests and leave them wanting more.

Serving: 4 servings
Preparation time: 10 minutes
Ready time: 20 minutes

Ingredients:
- 1 pound fresh scallops
- 4 tablespoons unsalted butter
- 4 cloves garlic, minced
- 1 tablespoon fresh parsley, chopped

- 1 tablespoon lemon juice
- Salt and pepper to taste

Instructions:
1. Rinse the scallops under cold water and pat them dry with a paper towel. Season them with salt and pepper on both sides.
2. In a large skillet, melt the butter over medium heat. Add the minced garlic and cook for 1-2 minutes until fragrant.
3. Increase the heat to medium-high and add the scallops to the skillet. Cook for 2-3 minutes on each side until they are golden brown and cooked through. Be careful not to overcook them as they can become tough and rubbery.
4. Remove the scallops from the skillet and set them aside on a plate.
5. Reduce the heat to low and add the lemon juice and chopped parsley to the skillet. Stir well to combine.
6. Return the scallops to the skillet and toss them in the garlic butter sauce until they are evenly coated.
7. Remove from heat and serve the scallops with the garlic butter sauce drizzled over the top.

Nutrition information per Serving: - Calories: 250
- Fat: 15g
- Carbohydrates: 5g
- Protein: 25g
- Fiber: 0g
- Sugar: 0g
- Sodium: 400mg

Note: Nutrition information may vary depending on the size of the scallops used and the amount of butter and garlic used in the recipe.

30. Chicken Fajitas

Chicken fajitas are a delicious and flavorful Mexican dish that is perfect for a quick and easy weeknight dinner. This recipe combines tender chicken, colorful bell peppers, and onions, all seasoned with a blend of spices and served in warm tortillas. With its vibrant flavors and customizable toppings, chicken fajitas are sure to be a hit with the whole family.

Serving: 4 servings
Preparation time: 15 minutes
Ready time: 25 minutes

Ingredients:
- 1 pound boneless, skinless chicken breasts, sliced into thin strips
- 2 tablespoons olive oil
- 1 red bell pepper, sliced
- 1 green bell pepper, sliced
- 1 yellow bell pepper, sliced
- 1 onion, sliced
- 2 cloves garlic, minced
- 1 teaspoon chili powder
- 1 teaspoon cumin
- 1/2 teaspoon paprika
- 1/2 teaspoon salt
- 1/4 teaspoon black pepper
- 1/4 teaspoon cayenne pepper (optional, for extra heat)
- 8 small flour tortillas
- Optional toppings: shredded cheese, sour cream, guacamole, salsa, chopped cilantro

Instructions:
1. In a large skillet, heat the olive oil over medium-high heat. Add the chicken strips and cook until browned and cooked through, about 5-6 minutes. Remove the chicken from the skillet and set aside.
2. In the same skillet, add the sliced bell peppers and onion. Cook for 4-5 minutes, until the vegetables are tender-crisp.
3. Add the minced garlic, chili powder, cumin, paprika, salt, black pepper, and cayenne pepper (if using) to the skillet. Stir well to coat the vegetables with the spices.
4. Return the cooked chicken to the skillet and toss with the vegetables and spices. Cook for an additional 2-3 minutes, until everything is heated through.
5. Warm the flour tortillas in a dry skillet or in the microwave.
6. To serve, spoon the chicken and vegetable mixture onto the warm tortillas. Add any desired toppings, such as shredded cheese, sour cream, guacamole, salsa, or chopped cilantro.
7. Roll up the tortillas and enjoy!

Nutrition information:
- Calories: 350
- Fat: 12g
- Carbohydrates: 32g
- Protein: 28g
- Fiber: 4g
- Sugar: 5g
- Sodium: 550mg

31. Smoked Haddock Kedgeree

Smoked Haddock Kedgeree is a classic British dish that combines the smoky flavors of haddock with fragrant spices and rice. This dish originated in colonial India and has since become a popular breakfast or brunch option. The combination of flaky fish, aromatic spices, and creamy rice makes it a satisfying and flavorful meal.

Serving: 4 servings
Preparation time: 15 minutes
Ready time: 30 minutes

Ingredients:
- 300g smoked haddock fillets
- 200g basmati rice
- 1 onion, finely chopped
- 2 cloves of garlic, minced
- 1 teaspoon curry powder
- 1 teaspoon turmeric
- 1 teaspoon cumin
- 1 teaspoon coriander
- 1 tablespoon vegetable oil
- 2 eggs, hard-boiled and chopped
- Fresh cilantro, chopped (for garnish)
- Salt and pepper to taste

Instructions:
1. In a large pan, bring water to a boil and add the smoked haddock fillets. Simmer for 5-7 minutes until the fish is cooked through. Remove

the fish from the water and set aside to cool. Once cooled, flake the fish into small pieces, discarding any skin or bones.

2. In a separate pot, cook the basmati rice according to the package instructions. Once cooked, set aside.

3. In a large skillet, heat the vegetable oil over medium heat. Add the chopped onion and minced garlic, and sauté until they become translucent and fragrant.

4. Add the curry powder, turmeric, cumin, and coriander to the skillet. Stir well to coat the onions and garlic with the spices.

5. Add the flaked smoked haddock to the skillet and stir gently to combine with the spices. Cook for an additional 2-3 minutes to allow the flavors to meld together.

6. Add the cooked basmati rice to the skillet and mix well, ensuring that the rice is evenly coated with the spices and fish. Season with salt and pepper to taste.

7. Finally, add the chopped hard-boiled eggs to the skillet and gently fold them into the rice mixture.

8. Serve the Smoked Haddock Kedgeree hot, garnished with fresh cilantro.

Nutrition information:
- Calories: 350 per Serving: - Fat: 8g
- Carbohydrates: 45g
- Protein: 25g
- Fiber: 2g

32. Lamb Kofta Kebabs

Lamb Kofta Kebabs are a delicious and easy-to-make Middle Eastern dish made with seasoned ground lamb formed into kebabs and grilled on skewers.

Serving: 4 servings
Preparation time: 20 minutes
Ready time: 30 minutes

Ingredients:
- 1 lb ground lamb
- 1/4 cup chopped onions

- 2 garlic cloves, minced
- 2 tablespoons chopped parsley
- 2 teaspoons fresh chopped mint
- 1 teaspoon ground cumin
- 1 teaspoon paprika
- 1/4 teaspoon cayenne pepper
- Salt and pepper, to taste
- 2 tablespoons olive oil

Instructions:
1. Preheat a grill or grill pan to medium-high heat.
2. In a large bowl, mix together the ground lamb, onion, garlic, parsley, mint, cumin, paprika, cayenne, salt and pepper.
3. Form the mixture into 8-10 small patties, and thread onto 4 skewers. Brush the kebabs with the olive oil.
4. Place the kebabs onto the grill and cook for 5-6 minutes per side, flipping once, until the kebabs are cooked through, about 10-12 minutes total.
5. Remove the kebabs from the heat and serve hot.

Nutrition information:
- Calories: 319
- Fat: 17 g
- Carbohydrates: 6 g
- Protein: 33 g

33. Baked Cod with Lemon Butter

Baked Cod with Lemon Butter is a delicious and healthy seafood dish that is perfect for any occasion. The combination of tender cod fillets, tangy lemon butter sauce, and aromatic herbs creates a mouthwatering flavor that will leave you wanting more. This recipe is quick and easy to prepare, making it a great option for busy weeknight dinners or special gatherings.
Serving: 4 servings
Preparation time: 10 minutes
Ready time: 25 minutes

Ingredients:
- 4 cod fillets (about 6 ounces each)
- 4 tablespoons unsalted butter, melted
- 2 tablespoons fresh lemon juice
- 2 cloves garlic, minced
- 1 teaspoon dried thyme
- 1 teaspoon dried parsley
- Salt and black pepper, to taste
- Lemon slices, for garnish
- Fresh parsley, for garnish

Instructions:
1. Preheat the oven to 400°F (200°C). Grease a baking dish with cooking spray or olive oil.
2. Place the cod fillets in the prepared baking dish, ensuring they are evenly spaced.
3. In a small bowl, combine the melted butter, lemon juice, minced garlic, dried thyme, dried parsley, salt, and black pepper. Stir well to combine.
4. Pour the lemon butter mixture over the cod fillets, making sure they are fully coated.
5. Place the baking dish in the preheated oven and bake for 15-20 minutes, or until the cod is opaque and flakes easily with a fork.
6. Remove the baking dish from the oven and let the cod rest for a few minutes.
7. Serve the baked cod with lemon butter hot, garnished with lemon slices and fresh parsley.

Nutrition information:
- Calories: 250
- Fat: 12g
- Carbohydrates: 2g
- Protein: 32g
- Fiber: 0g
- Sugar: 0g
- Sodium: 200mg
Note: Nutrition information may vary depending on the specific Ingredients and brands used.

34. Chicken Cordon Bleu

Chicken Cordon Bleu is a classic dish that combines tender chicken breast, savory ham, and gooey cheese, all wrapped up in a crispy breadcrumb coating. This elegant and delicious meal is sure to impress your family and friends.

Serving: 4 servings
Preparation time: 20 minutes
Ready time: 40 minutes

Ingredients:
- 4 boneless, skinless chicken breasts
- 4 slices of ham
- 4 slices of Swiss cheese
- 1 cup breadcrumbs
- 1/2 cup all-purpose flour
- 2 eggs, beaten
- Salt and pepper to taste
- Cooking oil for frying

Instructions:
1. Preheat your oven to 375°F (190°C).
2. Lay the chicken breasts flat on a cutting board and season them with salt and pepper.
3. Place a slice of ham and a slice of Swiss cheese on top of each chicken breast.
4. Roll up the chicken breasts tightly, making sure the filling is secure inside.
5. In three separate bowls, place the flour, beaten eggs, and breadcrumbs.
6. Dip each rolled chicken breast into the flour, then the beaten eggs, and finally coat it with breadcrumbs, pressing gently to adhere.
7. Heat cooking oil in a large skillet over medium-high heat.
8. Carefully place the breaded chicken breasts into the hot oil and cook for about 3-4 minutes on each side, or until golden brown.
9. Transfer the chicken breasts to a baking dish and bake in the preheated oven for 20-25 minutes, or until the chicken is cooked through and the cheese is melted and bubbly.
10. Remove from the oven and let the chicken rest for a few minutes before serving.

Nutrition information per Serving: - Calories: 450
- Fat: 20g
- Carbohydrates: 20g
- Protein: 45g
- Fiber: 2g

35. Irish Whiskey Cake

Irish Whiskey Cake is a rich and moist dessert that combines the flavors of whiskey, dried fruits, and warm spices. This traditional Irish treat is perfect for special occasions or as a delightful indulgence any time of the year. The whiskey adds a unique depth of flavor to the cake, making it a true crowd-pleaser.
Serving: 10-12 servings
Preparation time: 30 minutes
Ready time: 1 hour 30 minutes

Ingredients:
- 1 cup unsalted butter, softened
- 1 cup granulated sugar
- 4 large eggs
- 2 cups all-purpose flour
- 1 teaspoon baking powder
- 1/2 teaspoon baking soda
- 1/2 teaspoon salt
- 1 teaspoon ground cinnamon
- 1/2 teaspoon ground nutmeg
- 1/4 teaspoon ground cloves
- 1/2 cup Irish whiskey
- 1 cup mixed dried fruits (such as raisins, currants, and chopped dates)
- 1/2 cup chopped walnuts or pecans (optional)
- 1/2 cup buttermilk

Instructions:
1. Preheat your oven to 350°F (175°C). Grease and flour a 9-inch round cake pan or line it with parchment paper.
2. In a large mixing bowl, cream together the softened butter and granulated sugar until light and fluffy.

3. Add the eggs, one at a time, beating well after each addition.
4. In a separate bowl, whisk together the flour, baking powder, baking soda, salt, cinnamon, nutmeg, and cloves.
5. Gradually add the dry Ingredients to the butter mixture, alternating with the Irish whiskey. Begin and end with the dry Ingredients.
6. Stir in the dried fruits and chopped nuts (if using), followed by the buttermilk. Mix until just combined.
7. Pour the batter into the prepared cake pan and smooth the top with a spatula.
8. Bake for approximately 1 hour and 15 minutes, or until a toothpick inserted into the center comes out clean.
9. Remove the cake from the oven and let it cool in the pan for 10 minutes. Then, transfer it to a wire rack to cool completely.
10. Once cooled, you can serve the Irish Whiskey Cake as is or dust it with powdered sugar for an extra touch of sweetness.

Nutrition information per Serving: - Calories: 350
- Fat: 18g
- Carbohydrates: 40g
- Protein: 5g
- Fiber: 2g
- Sugar: 22g
- Sodium: 250mg
Note: The nutrition information provided is an estimate and may vary depending on the specific Ingredients used.

36. Beef and Vegetable Stir-Fry

This Beef and Vegetable Stir-Fry is an easy and delicious dish perfect for creating a quickAsian-inspired meal with a few simple Ingredients.
Serving: 4
Preparation time: 20 minutes
Ready time: 30 minutes

Ingredients:
- 2 tablespoons vegetable oil
- 2 cloves garlic, minced
- 500g diced beef stir-fry steak

- 2 tablespoons cornflour
- 1 teaspoon soy sauce
- 400g mixed vegetables, sliced or diced
- 3 tablespoons oyster sauce

Instructions:
1. Heat oil in a wok or large heavy-based frypan over high heat.
2. Add garlic and beef and stir-fry for 2 minutes until beef is lightly browned.
3. Combine cornflour, soy sauce and 2 tablespoons cold water then add to the pan. Stir-fry for 1 minute.
4. Add vegetables and oyster sauce and stir-fry for 2–3 minutes until vegetables are just tender.
5. Serve with steamed rice.

Nutrition information:
Calories: 400
Fat: 16g
Carbohydrates: 29g
Protein: 34g
Sodium: 600mg

37. Shrimp Scampi

Shrimp Scampi is a classic Italian-American dish that features succulent shrimp cooked in a flavorful garlic and butter sauce. This dish is quick and easy to prepare, making it perfect for a weeknight dinner or a special occasion. The combination of garlic, lemon, and white wine creates a deliciously tangy and aromatic sauce that pairs perfectly with the tender shrimp. Serve this dish with pasta or crusty bread to soak up all the delicious flavors.
Serving: 4 servings
Preparation time: 10 minutes
Ready time: 20 minutes

Ingredients:
- 1 pound large shrimp, peeled and deveined
- 4 tablespoons unsalted butter

- 4 cloves garlic, minced
- 1/4 cup white wine
- 2 tablespoons freshly squeezed lemon juice
- 1/4 teaspoon red pepper flakes (optional)
- Salt and black pepper, to taste
- 2 tablespoons chopped fresh parsley
- Lemon wedges, for Serving:

Instructions:
1. In a large skillet, melt the butter over medium heat. Add the minced garlic and cook for 1-2 minutes until fragrant.
2. Increase the heat to medium-high and add the shrimp to the skillet. Cook for 2-3 minutes on each side until the shrimp turn pink and opaque.
3. Remove the shrimp from the skillet and set aside.
4. Pour the white wine and lemon juice into the skillet, scraping the bottom to deglaze the pan. Cook for 2-3 minutes until the liquid has reduced slightly.
5. Add the red pepper flakes (if using), salt, and black pepper to the skillet. Stir well to combine.
6. Return the cooked shrimp to the skillet and toss to coat them in the sauce. Cook for an additional 1-2 minutes until the shrimp are heated through.
7. Remove the skillet from the heat and sprinkle the chopped parsley over the shrimp scampi.
8. Serve the shrimp scampi hot with lemon wedges on the side.

Nutrition information:
- Calories: 250
- Fat: 14g
- Carbohydrates: 3g
- Protein: 25g
- Fiber: 0g
- Sugar: 0g
- Sodium: 350mg

38. Salmon en Croute

Salmon en Croute is a delicious and elegant dish that combines the rich flavors of salmon with a flaky puff pastry crust. This dish is perfect for special occasions or when you want to impress your guests with a gourmet meal. The salmon is seasoned with herbs and wrapped in puff pastry, creating a beautiful presentation and a mouthwatering taste. Serve it with a side of fresh vegetables or a light salad for a complete and satisfying meal.

Serving: 4 servings
Preparation time: 20 minutes
Ready time: 40 minutes

Ingredients:
- 4 salmon fillets (about 6 ounces each)
- Salt and pepper, to taste
- 1 tablespoon fresh dill, chopped
- 1 tablespoon fresh parsley, chopped
- 1 tablespoon fresh lemon juice
- 1 sheet puff pastry, thawed
- 1 egg, beaten (for egg wash)

Instructions:
1. Preheat your oven to 400°F (200°C). Line a baking sheet with parchment paper.
2. Season the salmon fillets with salt, pepper, dill, parsley, and lemon juice. Set aside.
3. On a lightly floured surface, roll out the puff pastry sheet to a thickness of about 1/8 inch.
4. Cut the puff pastry into four equal squares, large enough to wrap each salmon fillet.
5. Place a seasoned salmon fillet in the center of each puff pastry square.
6. Fold the puff pastry over the salmon, sealing the edges by pressing them together with your fingers.
7. Place the wrapped salmon fillets on the prepared baking sheet, seam side down.
8. Brush the top of each pastry-wrapped salmon with the beaten egg wash.
9. Bake in the preheated oven for about 20-25 minutes, or until the puff pastry is golden brown and the salmon is cooked through.
10. Remove from the oven and let it rest for a few minutes before serving.

Nutrition information per Serving: - Calories: 450
- Fat: 28g
- Protein: 32g
- Carbohydrates: 18g
- Fiber: 1g
- Sugar: 0g
- Sodium: 350mg
Note: Nutrition information may vary depending on the specific
Ingredients and brands used.

39. Chicken Curry

Chicken curry is a delicious and aromatic dish that is loved by many. This
flavorful curry is made with tender chicken pieces cooked in a rich and
creamy sauce, infused with a blend of spices. It is a perfect dish to serve
with steamed rice or naan bread, and it is sure to satisfy your taste buds.
Serving:
This recipe serves 4 people.
Preparation time:
Preparation time for this chicken curry is approximately 15 minutes.
Ready time:
The chicken curry will be ready to serve in about 45 minutes.

Ingredients:
- 500 grams boneless chicken, cut into bite-sized pieces
- 2 tablespoons vegetable oil
- 1 large onion, finely chopped
- 3 cloves of garlic, minced
- 1-inch piece of ginger, grated
- 2 teaspoons curry powder
- 1 teaspoon ground cumin
- 1 teaspoon ground coriander
- 1/2 teaspoon turmeric powder
- 1/2 teaspoon chili powder (adjust according to your spice preference)
- 1 cup coconut milk
- 1 cup tomato puree
- Salt to taste

- Fresh cilantro leaves for garnish

Instructions:
1. Heat the vegetable oil in a large pan over medium heat. Add the chopped onion and sauté until it becomes translucent.
2. Add the minced garlic and grated ginger to the pan and cook for another minute, stirring continuously.
3. In a small bowl, mix together the curry powder, ground cumin, ground coriander, turmeric powder, and chili powder. Add this spice mixture to the pan and cook for a minute, stirring well to coat the onions, garlic, and ginger with the spices.
4. Add the chicken pieces to the pan and cook until they are browned on all sides.
5. Pour in the coconut milk and tomato puree, and season with salt. Stir well to combine all the Ingredients.
6. Reduce the heat to low, cover the pan, and let the curry simmer for about 30 minutes, or until the chicken is cooked through and tender.
7. Once the chicken is cooked, remove the lid and let the curry simmer for another 5 minutes to thicken the sauce slightly.
8. Garnish with fresh cilantro leaves before serving.

Nutrition information per Serving: - Calories: 320
- Fat: 20g
- Carbohydrates: 10g
- Protein: 25g
- Fiber: 2g
Note: The nutrition information provided is an estimate and may vary depending on the specific Ingredients used.

40. Irish Colcannon

Irish Colcannon is a traditional Irish dish that combines creamy mashed potatoes with tender cabbage or kale. This comforting and hearty dish is perfect for St. Patrick's Day or any time you're craving a taste of Ireland. The combination of flavors and textures in this dish is sure to please your taste buds and leave you feeling satisfied.
Serving: 4 servings
Preparation time: 15 minutes

Ready time: 30 minutes

Ingredients:
- 4 large potatoes, peeled and cut into chunks
- 4 cups cabbage or kale, finely shredded
- 1/2 cup milk
- 4 tablespoons butter
- Salt and pepper to taste
- Optional: 4 slices of bacon, cooked and crumbled

Instructions:
1. Place the potatoes in a large pot and cover with water. Bring to a boil over high heat and cook until the potatoes are tender when pierced with a fork, about 15 minutes.
2. While the potatoes are cooking, melt 2 tablespoons of butter in a separate pan over medium heat. Add the cabbage or kale and sauté until wilted and tender, about 5 minutes. Remove from heat and set aside.
3. Drain the cooked potatoes and return them to the pot. Add the milk and remaining butter. Mash the potatoes until smooth and creamy. Season with salt and pepper to taste.
4. Stir in the sautéed cabbage or kale into the mashed potatoes until well combined. If desired, sprinkle the crumbled bacon on top.
5. Serve the Irish Colcannon hot as a side dish with your favorite main course. It pairs well with roasted meats or can be enjoyed on its own.

Nutrition information per Serving: - Calories: 250
- Fat: 12g
- Carbohydrates: 32g
- Protein: 5g
- Fiber: 4g
Note: Nutrition information may vary depending on the specific Ingredients and brands used.

41. Beef Tacos

Beef Tacos are a delicious and popular Mexican dish that is loved by people all around the world. These tacos are filled with flavorful seasoned beef, topped with fresh Ingredients, and wrapped in a warm tortilla. They are perfect for a quick and satisfying meal that the whole family will enjoy.

Serving: 4 servings

Preparation time: 15 minutes

Ready time: 30 minutes

Ingredients:

- 1 pound ground beef
- 1 tablespoon olive oil
- 1 small onion, diced
- 2 cloves garlic, minced
- 1 tablespoon chili powder
- 1 teaspoon cumin
- 1 teaspoon paprika
- 1/2 teaspoon salt
- 1/4 teaspoon black pepper
- 1/4 cup tomato sauce
- 1/4 cup water
- 8 small flour tortillas
- 1 cup shredded lettuce
- 1 cup diced tomatoes
- 1/2 cup shredded cheddar cheese
- 1/4 cup chopped fresh cilantro
- Sour cream and salsa, for serving (optional)

Instructions:

1. In a large skillet, heat the olive oil over medium heat. Add the diced onion and minced garlic, and sauté until they become translucent and fragrant, about 2-3 minutes.

2. Add the ground beef to the skillet and cook, breaking it up with a spoon, until it is browned and cooked through, about 5-7 minutes.

3. Drain any excess fat from the skillet, then add the chili powder, cumin, paprika, salt, and black pepper. Stir well to coat the beef with the spices.

4. Pour in the tomato sauce and water, and stir to combine. Reduce the heat to low and let the beef simmer for 10-15 minutes, allowing the flavors to meld together.

5. While the beef is simmering, warm the flour tortillas in a dry skillet or microwave according to package instructions.

6. To assemble the tacos, spoon a generous amount of the beef mixture onto each tortilla. Top with shredded lettuce, diced tomatoes, shredded cheddar cheese, and chopped cilantro.

7. Serve the beef tacos with sour cream and salsa on the side, if desired.

Nutrition information:
- Calories: 450
- Fat: 22g
- Carbohydrates: 35g
- Protein: 28g
- Fiber: 4g
- Sugar: 3g
- Sodium: 650mg

Note: Nutrition information may vary depending on the specific Ingredients and brands used.

42. Crab Cakes with Remoulade Sauce

This recipe is a classic crab cake classic served with a classic remoulade sauce. This dish is perfect for entertaining guests, as it is easy to make and can be prepared ahead of time. It is filled with flavor and always succeeds to impress.

Serving: 6-8
Preparation Time: 20 minutes
Ready Time: 1 hour

Ingredients:
Crab Cakes:
• 1 lb crabmeat
• 2 tablespoons olive oil
• 1 large egg
• 2 tablespoons Dijon mustard
• 1 teaspoon Worcestershire sauce
• 1/4 cup mayonnaise
• 1 1/2 tablespoons lemon juice
• 1/4 cup green onion, minced
• 2 cloves garlic, minced
• 2 tablespoons fresh parsley, chopped

- 2/3 cup panko bread crumbs

Remoulade Sauce:
- 1/3 cup mayonnaise
- 1 tablespoon Dijon mustard
- 1 tablespoon horseradish
- 2 tablespoons lemon juice
- 1/4 teaspoon paprika
- 1 teaspoon Worcestershire sauce
- 2 tablespoons capers, chopped
- 2 tablespoons fresh parsley, chopped
- 2 tablespoons sweet relish

Instructions:

1. Combine all the crab cake Ingredients together in a bowl and stir until well blended. Form into 4-5 inch patties and place on a lightly greased baking sheet.

2. Bake in the preheated oven for 15 minutes, or until golden brown.

3. To make the remoulade sauce, combine all the Ingredients in a bowl. Serve over the crab cakes.

Nutrition information:

Serving Size: 1 crab cake with 2 tablespoons of remoulade sauce
Calories: 126
Fat: 9 g
Carbohydrates: 8 g
Protein: 4 g
Sodium: 360 mg

43. Lamb Rogan Josh

Lamb Rogan Josh is a classic Indian dish that is known for its rich and aromatic flavors. This slow-cooked curry is made with tender pieces of lamb cooked in a flavorful blend of spices, yogurt, and tomatoes. It is a perfect dish to warm up your taste buds and satisfy your cravings for a hearty and delicious meal.

Serving: 4 servings
Preparation time: 15 minutes
Ready time: 2 hours 30 minutes

Ingredients:
- 500 grams lamb, cut into bite-sized pieces
- 2 tablespoons vegetable oil
- 2 onions, finely chopped
- 4 cloves of garlic, minced
- 1-inch piece of ginger, grated
- 2 teaspoons ground cumin
- 2 teaspoons ground coriander
- 1 teaspoon ground turmeric
- 1 teaspoon paprika
- 1 teaspoon chili powder (adjust according to your spice preference)
- 1 cup plain yogurt
- 2 tomatoes, pureed
- 1 cup water
- Salt, to taste
- Fresh cilantro, for garnish

Instructions:
1. Heat the vegetable oil in a large, deep pan over medium heat. Add the chopped onions and cook until they turn golden brown, stirring occasionally.
2. Add the minced garlic and grated ginger to the pan and cook for another 2 minutes, until fragrant.
3. In a small bowl, mix together the ground cumin, coriander, turmeric, paprika, and chili powder. Add this spice mixture to the pan and cook for 1 minute, stirring constantly.
4. Add the lamb pieces to the pan and cook until they are browned on all sides, about 5 minutes.
5. Reduce the heat to low and add the plain yogurt to the pan. Stir well to coat the lamb with the yogurt and cook for 2 minutes.
6. Pour in the pureed tomatoes and water, and season with salt to taste. Stir everything together, cover the pan, and simmer for 2 hours, or until the lamb is tender and the flavors have melded together.
7. Once the lamb is cooked, garnish with fresh cilantro and serve hot with steamed rice or naan bread.

Nutrition information:
- Calories: 350 per Serving: - Fat: 20g
- Carbohydrates: 10g

- Protein: 30g
- Fiber: 2g

44. Grilled Swordfish with Chimichurri Sauce

Grilled Swordfish with Chimichurri Sauce is a delicious and healthy dish that combines the smoky flavors of grilled swordfish with the vibrant and tangy flavors of chimichurri sauce. This recipe is perfect for a summer barbecue or a special dinner. The swordfish is marinated in a simple mixture of olive oil, lemon juice, and herbs, then grilled to perfection. The chimichurri sauce, made with fresh herbs, garlic, vinegar, and olive oil, adds a burst of flavor to the dish. Serve this Grilled Swordfish with Chimichurri Sauce with a side of grilled vegetables or a fresh salad for a complete and satisfying meal.
Serving: 4 servings
Preparation time: 15 minutes
Ready time: 30 minutes

Ingredients:
- 4 swordfish steaks (about 6 ounces each)
- 1/4 cup olive oil
- 2 tablespoons lemon juice
- 2 cloves garlic, minced
- 1 teaspoon dried oregano
- Salt and pepper to taste
For the Chimichurri Sauce:
- 1 cup fresh parsley, finely chopped
- 1/4 cup fresh cilantro, finely chopped
- 2 cloves garlic, minced
- 2 tablespoons red wine vinegar
- 1/2 cup olive oil
- Salt and pepper to taste

Instructions:
1. In a small bowl, whisk together the olive oil, lemon juice, minced garlic, dried oregano, salt, and pepper. Place the swordfish steaks in a shallow dish and pour the marinade over them. Let the swordfish marinate for at least 15 minutes, turning once.

2. While the swordfish is marinating, prepare the chimichurri sauce. In a medium bowl, combine the chopped parsley, cilantro, minced garlic, red wine vinegar, olive oil, salt, and pepper. Stir well to combine. Set aside.

3. Preheat the grill to medium-high heat. Remove the swordfish steaks from the marinade and discard the marinade. Place the swordfish on the grill and cook for about 4-5 minutes per side, or until the fish is opaque and flakes easily with a fork.

4. Remove the swordfish from the grill and let it rest for a few minutes. Serve the grilled swordfish steaks with a generous spoonful of chimichurri sauce on top. Enjoy!

Nutrition information per Serving: - Calories: 350
- Fat: 25g
- Protein: 30g
- Carbohydrates: 2g
- Fiber: 1g
- Sugar: 0g
- Sodium: 150mg

45. Chicken Satay with Peanut Sauce

Chicken Satay with Peanut Sauce is a popular Southeast Asian dish that is loved for its flavorful and tender chicken skewers served with a rich and creamy peanut sauce. This dish is perfect for parties, barbecues, or even as a main course for a weeknight dinner. The combination of juicy chicken and the nutty and slightly spicy peanut sauce is simply irresistible.

Serving:
This recipe serves 4 people.
Preparation time:
Preparation time for this dish is approximately 20 minutes.
Ready time:
The total cooking time for Chicken Satay with Peanut Sauce is around 30 minutes.

Ingredients:
- 1 lb (450g) boneless, skinless chicken breasts, cut into thin strips
- 1/4 cup soy sauce

- 2 tablespoons honey
- 2 tablespoons vegetable oil
- 2 cloves garlic, minced
- 1 teaspoon ground coriander
- 1/2 teaspoon ground cumin
- 1/4 teaspoon turmeric
- 1/4 teaspoon chili powder (optional, for added heat)
- Wooden skewers, soaked in water for 30 minutes before grilling

For the Peanut Sauce:
- 1/2 cup creamy peanut butter
- 1/4 cup coconut milk
- 2 tablespoons soy sauce
- 1 tablespoon honey
- 1 tablespoon lime juice
- 1 clove garlic, minced
- 1/2 teaspoon ground ginger
- 1/4 teaspoon chili flakes (optional, for added heat)
- Chopped peanuts and fresh cilantro, for garnish

Instructions:

1. In a bowl, combine soy sauce, honey, vegetable oil, minced garlic, ground coriander, ground cumin, turmeric, and chili powder (if using). Mix well to make the marinade.

2. Add the chicken strips to the marinade and toss to coat evenly. Allow the chicken to marinate for at least 1 hour, or overnight in the refrigerator for maximum flavor.

3. Preheat your grill or grill pan over medium-high heat.

4. Thread the marinated chicken strips onto the soaked wooden skewers.

5. Grill the chicken skewers for about 3-4 minutes per side, or until cooked through and slightly charred. Make sure to turn them occasionally for even cooking.

6. While the chicken is grilling, prepare the peanut sauce. In a small saucepan, combine peanut butter, coconut milk, soy sauce, honey, lime juice, minced garlic, ground ginger, and chili flakes (if using). Cook over low heat, stirring constantly, until the sauce is smooth and heated through.

7. Once the chicken skewers are cooked, remove them from the grill and let them rest for a few minutes.

8. Serve the Chicken Satay with Peanut Sauce on a platter, garnished with chopped peanuts and fresh cilantro. Serve the peanut sauce on the side for dipping.

Nutrition information:
- Calories: 350
- Fat: 18g
- Carbohydrates: 15g
- Protein: 32g
- Fiber: 2g
- Sugar: 9g
- Sodium: 800mg

Note: Nutrition information may vary depending on the specific brands and quantities of Ingredients used.

46. Irish Apple Cake

Irish Apple Cake is a delicious and comforting dessert that combines the flavors of sweet apples, warm spices, and a buttery cake. This traditional Irish treat is perfect for any occasion, whether it's a cozy family dinner or a St. Patrick's Day celebration. With its moist texture and irresistible aroma, this apple cake is sure to become a favorite in your household.

Serving: 8 servings
Preparation time: 20 minutes
Ready time: 1 hour 30 minutes

Ingredients:
- 2 cups all-purpose flour
- 1 teaspoon baking powder
- 1/2 teaspoon baking soda
- 1/2 teaspoon ground cinnamon
- 1/4 teaspoon ground nutmeg
- 1/4 teaspoon salt
- 1/2 cup unsalted butter, softened
- 1 cup granulated sugar
- 2 large eggs
- 1 teaspoon vanilla extract
- 1/2 cup buttermilk

- 2 cups peeled, cored, and diced apples (about 2 medium-sized apples)
- 1/4 cup granulated sugar (for topping)
- 1/2 teaspoon ground cinnamon (for topping)

Instructions:
1. Preheat your oven to 350°F (175°C). Grease and flour a 9-inch round cake pan.
2. In a medium bowl, whisk together the flour, baking powder, baking soda, cinnamon, nutmeg, and salt. Set aside.
3. In a large mixing bowl, cream together the softened butter and sugar until light and fluffy. Add the eggs, one at a time, beating well after each addition. Stir in the vanilla extract.
4. Gradually add the dry Ingredients to the butter mixture, alternating with the buttermilk. Begin and end with the dry Ingredients, mixing just until combined.
5. Gently fold in the diced apples until evenly distributed throughout the batter.
6. Pour the batter into the prepared cake pan, spreading it out evenly.
7. In a small bowl, combine the 1/4 cup of granulated sugar and 1/2 teaspoon of cinnamon for the topping. Sprinkle this mixture evenly over the top of the cake batter.
8. Bake in the preheated oven for 50-60 minutes, or until a toothpick inserted into the center comes out clean.
9. Allow the cake to cool in the pan for 10 minutes, then transfer it to a wire rack to cool completely.
10. Serve the Irish Apple Cake warm or at room temperature. It can be enjoyed on its own or with a dollop of whipped cream or a scoop of vanilla ice cream.

Nutrition information (per serving):
- Calories: 320
- Fat: 12g
- Carbohydrates: 50g
- Fiber: 2g
- Sugar: 29g
- Protein: 4g
- Sodium: 220mg

47. Beef Stir-Fry with Broccoli

Beef Stir-Fry with Broccoli is a delicious and nutritious dish that combines tender beef strips with crisp broccoli florets in a savory sauce. This quick and easy recipe is perfect for busy weeknights when you want a healthy and satisfying meal on the table in no time.

Serving: 4 servings
Preparation time: 15 minutes
Ready time: 25 minutes

Ingredients:
- 1 lb beef sirloin, thinly sliced
- 2 cups broccoli florets
- 1 red bell pepper, thinly sliced
- 1 onion, thinly sliced
- 3 cloves garlic, minced
- 2 tablespoons soy sauce
- 1 tablespoon oyster sauce
- 1 tablespoon cornstarch
- 1 teaspoon sesame oil
- 2 tablespoons vegetable oil
- Salt and pepper to taste

Instructions:
1. In a small bowl, whisk together soy sauce, oyster sauce, cornstarch, and sesame oil. Set aside.
2. Heat vegetable oil in a large skillet or wok over medium-high heat.
3. Add beef slices to the skillet and stir-fry for 2-3 minutes until browned. Remove beef from the skillet and set aside.
4. In the same skillet, add garlic, onion, and bell pepper. Stir-fry for 2-3 minutes until vegetables are slightly tender.
5. Add broccoli florets to the skillet and continue stir-frying for another 2 minutes.
6. Return the beef to the skillet and pour the sauce mixture over the Ingredients. Stir well to coat everything evenly.
7. Cook for an additional 2-3 minutes until the sauce thickens and coats the beef and vegetables.
8. Season with salt and pepper to taste.
9. Remove from heat and serve hot over steamed rice or noodles.

Nutrition information per Serving: - Calories: 320
- Protein: 28g
- Fat: 15g
- Carbohydrates: 20g
- Fiber: 4g
- Sugar: 6g
- Sodium: 800mg
Note: Nutrition information may vary depending on the specific
Ingredients and brands used.

48. Shrimp and Grits

Shrimp and Grits is a classic Southern dish that combines succulent
shrimp with creamy grits. This comforting and flavorful meal is perfect
for breakfast, brunch, or even dinner. The combination of tender shrimp
and creamy grits creates a harmonious balance of flavors that will leave
you craving for more.
Serving: 4 servings
Preparation time: 10 minutes
Ready time: 30 minutes

Ingredients:
- 1 pound of fresh shrimp, peeled and deveined
- 1 cup of stone-ground grits
- 4 cups of water
- 1 cup of shredded cheddar cheese
- 4 slices of bacon, cooked and crumbled
- 1 small onion, finely chopped
- 2 cloves of garlic, minced
- 1 tablespoon of butter
- 1 tablespoon of olive oil
- 1 tablespoon of Cajun seasoning
- Salt and pepper to taste
- Fresh parsley, chopped (for garnish)

Instructions:

1. In a medium-sized saucepan, bring the water to a boil. Slowly whisk in the grits and reduce the heat to low. Cook the grits for about 20 minutes, stirring occasionally, until they become thick and creamy.

2. Stir in the shredded cheddar cheese until melted and well combined. Season with salt and pepper to taste. Set aside.

3. In a large skillet, heat the butter and olive oil over medium heat. Add the chopped onion and minced garlic, and sauté until the onion becomes translucent and fragrant.

4. Add the shrimp to the skillet and sprinkle with Cajun seasoning. Cook the shrimp for about 3-4 minutes on each side, or until they turn pink and opaque. Be careful not to overcook them, as they can become rubbery.

5. Once the shrimp are cooked, remove them from the skillet and set aside. In the same skillet, add the cooked and crumbled bacon, and sauté for a minute to warm it up.

6. To serve, spoon a generous amount of the creamy grits onto a plate or bowl. Top with the cooked shrimp and sprinkle with the bacon. Garnish with fresh parsley for added freshness and color.

7. Serve the Shrimp and Grits immediately while still hot and enjoy!

Nutrition information:
- Calories: 450
- Fat: 20g
- Carbohydrates: 30g
- Protein: 35g
- Fiber: 2g
- Sugar: 1g
- Sodium: 800mg

Note: Nutrition information may vary depending on the specific Ingredients and brands used.

49. Lemon Herb Roast Chicken

Lemon Herb Roast Chicken is a delicious and flavorful dish that is perfect for any occasion. The combination of zesty lemon and aromatic herbs creates a mouthwatering taste that will leave you wanting more. This recipe is easy to follow and will impress your family and friends with its tender and juicy chicken.

Serving: 4 servings
Preparation time: 15 minutes
Ready time: 1 hour 30 minutes

Ingredients:
- 1 whole chicken (about 4 pounds)
- 2 lemons
- 4 cloves of garlic, minced
- 2 tablespoons fresh rosemary, chopped
- 2 tablespoons fresh thyme, chopped
- 2 tablespoons fresh parsley, chopped
- 2 tablespoons olive oil
- Salt and pepper to taste

Instructions:
1. Preheat your oven to 375°F (190°C).
2. Rinse the chicken thoroughly under cold water and pat it dry with paper towels.
3. In a small bowl, combine the minced garlic, chopped rosemary, thyme, parsley, olive oil, salt, and pepper. Mix well to create a paste.
4. Carefully loosen the skin of the chicken by gently sliding your fingers between the skin and the meat. Be careful not to tear the skin.
5. Rub the herb paste all over the chicken, making sure to get some under the skin as well. This will help infuse the flavors into the meat.
6. Cut one lemon in half and squeeze the juice all over the chicken. Place the squeezed lemon halves inside the cavity of the chicken.
7. Slice the remaining lemon into thin rounds and arrange them on top of the chicken.
8. Place the chicken on a roasting rack in a roasting pan, breast side up.
9. Roast the chicken in the preheated oven for about 1 hour and 30 minutes, or until the internal temperature reaches 165°F (74°C) when measured with a meat thermometer inserted into the thickest part of the thigh.
10. Once cooked, remove the chicken from the oven and let it rest for 10 minutes before carving.
11. Serve the Lemon Herb Roast Chicken with your favorite side dishes and enjoy!

Nutrition information:
- Calories: 350 per Serving: - Fat: 18g

- Protein: 40g
- Carbohydrates: 4g
- Fiber: 1g
- Sugar: 1g
- Sodium: 150mg

50. Irish Coffee

Irish Coffee is a classic cocktail that combines the rich flavors of coffee, Irish whiskey, sugar, and cream. It is the perfect drink to warm you up on a chilly evening or to enjoy as a dessert after a delicious meal. The combination of the smooth whiskey and the bold coffee creates a delightful balance of flavors that is sure to please any coffee lover. So, grab your favorite mug and get ready to indulge in this delightful Irish treat!

Serving: 1 Serving: Preparation time: 5 minutes
Ready time: 5 minutes

Ingredients:
- 1 cup of freshly brewed hot coffee
- 1 ½ ounces of Irish whiskey
- 1 tablespoon of brown sugar
- Whipped cream, for topping

Instructions:
1. Start by brewing a fresh cup of hot coffee. Make sure it is strong and flavorful.
2. In a heatproof glass or mug, add the Irish whiskey and brown sugar.
3. Pour the hot coffee into the glass and stir until the sugar has dissolved completely.
4. Top the coffee with a generous amount of whipped cream. You can either spoon it on top or use a piping bag for a more decorative touch.
5. Optionally, you can sprinkle some cocoa powder or cinnamon on top of the whipped cream for added flavor and presentation.
6. Serve the Irish Coffee immediately while it is still hot. Enjoy!

Nutrition information:
- Calories: 180

- Fat: 6g
- Carbohydrates: 12g
- Protein: 1g
- Sugar: 9g
- Sodium: 5mg
- Caffeine: 95mg

Note: The nutrition information provided is an estimate and may vary depending on the specific Ingredients used.

51. Chicken and Mushroom Pie

Chicken and Mushroom Pie is a classic comfort food that combines tender chicken, earthy mushrooms, and a rich, creamy sauce, all encased in a flaky pastry crust. This hearty dish is perfect for a cozy dinner or a special occasion.

Serving: 6 servings
Preparation time: 30 minutes
Ready time: 1 hour 30 minutes

Ingredients:
- 2 cups cooked chicken, shredded or diced
- 1 cup mushrooms, sliced
- 1 onion, diced
- 2 cloves garlic, minced
- 2 tablespoons butter
- 2 tablespoons all-purpose flour
- 1 cup chicken broth
- 1 cup milk
- 1 teaspoon dried thyme
- Salt and pepper to taste
- 1 package store-bought puff pastry, thawed
- 1 egg, beaten (for egg wash)

Instructions:
1. Preheat your oven to 375°F (190°C).
2. In a large skillet, melt the butter over medium heat. Add the diced onion and minced garlic, and sauté until the onion becomes translucent.

3. Add the sliced mushrooms to the skillet and cook until they release their moisture and start to brown.

4. Sprinkle the flour over the mushroom mixture and stir well to coat everything evenly. Cook for another minute to cook off the raw flour taste.

5. Slowly pour in the chicken broth and milk, stirring constantly to prevent lumps from forming. Bring the mixture to a simmer and cook until it thickens, about 5 minutes.

6. Add the cooked chicken, dried thyme, salt, and pepper to the skillet. Stir well to combine all the Ingredients. Remove from heat and let the filling cool slightly.

7. Roll out the puff pastry on a lightly floured surface to fit your pie dish. Place the pastry over the dish, trimming any excess and crimping the edges to seal.

8. Brush the beaten egg over the pastry to give it a golden color when baked.

9. Cut a few slits on the top of the pastry to allow steam to escape during baking.

10. Place the pie dish on a baking sheet and bake in the preheated oven for 45-50 minutes, or until the pastry is golden brown and the filling is bubbling.

11. Remove from the oven and let the pie cool for a few minutes before serving.

Nutrition information per Serving: - Calories: 350

- Fat: 20g
- Carbohydrates: 25g
- Protein: 18g
- Fiber: 2g

Note: Nutrition information may vary depending on the specific Ingredients and brands used.

52. Seafood Linguine

Seafood Linguine is a delicious and flavorful pasta dish that combines the freshness of seafood with the richness of linguine pasta. This dish is perfect for seafood lovers and is sure to impress your family and friends.

With a creamy sauce and a medley of seafood, this linguine dish is a true crowd-pleaser.

Serving: 4 servings
Preparation time: 15 minutes
Ready time: 30 minutes

Ingredients:
- 8 ounces linguine pasta
- 1 tablespoon olive oil
- 4 cloves garlic, minced
- 1 small onion, finely chopped
- 1/2 cup white wine
- 1 cup heavy cream
- 1 cup seafood stock
- 1 pound mixed seafood (such as shrimp, scallops, and mussels)
- 1/4 cup grated Parmesan cheese
- Salt and pepper to taste
- Fresh parsley, chopped (for garnish)

Instructions:
1. Cook the linguine pasta according to the package instructions until al dente. Drain and set aside.
2. In a large skillet, heat the olive oil over medium heat. Add the minced garlic and chopped onion, and sauté until fragrant and translucent.
3. Pour in the white wine and let it simmer for a couple of minutes to cook off the alcohol.
4. Add the heavy cream and seafood stock to the skillet, and bring the mixture to a simmer. Let it cook for about 5 minutes, until the sauce thickens slightly.
5. Add the mixed seafood to the skillet and cook for another 5-7 minutes, or until the seafood is cooked through. Be careful not to overcook the seafood, as it can become tough.
6. Stir in the grated Parmesan cheese and season with salt and pepper to taste.
7. Add the cooked linguine pasta to the skillet and toss everything together until the pasta is well coated with the creamy seafood sauce.
8. Serve the Seafood Linguine hot, garnished with fresh parsley.

Nutrition information per Serving: - Calories: 520
- Fat: 25g

- Carbohydrates: 45g
- Protein: 30g
- Fiber: 2g

53. Corned Beef Hash

Corned Beef Hash is a classic comfort food that is perfect for breakfast or brunch. Made with tender corned beef, potatoes, and onions, this dish is hearty and flavorful. It's a great way to use up leftover corned beef from St. Patrick's Day or any other occasion. With a crispy exterior and a savory interior, Corned Beef Hash is sure to become a family favorite.
Serving: 4 servings
Preparation time: 15 minutes
Ready time: 30 minutes

Ingredients:
- 2 cups cooked corned beef, diced
- 2 cups potatoes, peeled and diced
- 1 medium onion, diced
- 2 tablespoons butter
- Salt and pepper to taste
- 1 teaspoon dried thyme
- 4 large eggs (optional)
- Fresh parsley for garnish (optional)

Instructions:
1. In a large skillet, melt the butter over medium heat. Add the diced onions and cook until they become translucent, about 5 minutes.
2. Add the diced potatoes to the skillet and cook until they are golden brown and crispy, stirring occasionally. This will take about 15 minutes.
3. Once the potatoes are cooked, add the diced corned beef to the skillet. Stir everything together and season with salt, pepper, and dried thyme. Cook for an additional 5 minutes to allow the flavors to meld together.
4. If desired, create four wells in the hash and crack an egg into each well. Cover the skillet and cook until the eggs are cooked to your liking. This will take about 5 minutes for a runny yolk or 8 minutes for a fully cooked yolk.

5. Remove the skillet from the heat and garnish with fresh parsley, if desired.
6. Serve the Corned Beef Hash hot and enjoy!

Nutrition information per Serving: - Calories: 350
- Fat: 18g
- Carbohydrates: 20g
- Protein: 25g
- Fiber: 2g
- Sugar: 2g
- Sodium: 900mg
Note: Nutrition information may vary depending on the specific Ingredients and brands used.

54. Beef Kebabs with Tzatziki Sauce

Beef Kebabs with Tzatziki Sauce is a delicious and flavorful dish that combines tender beef skewers with a creamy and tangy tzatziki sauce. This Mediterranean-inspired recipe is perfect for grilling season or any time you're craving a tasty and satisfying meal. The combination of juicy beef and refreshing tzatziki sauce will surely impress your family and friends.
Serving: 4 servings
Preparation time: 20 minutes
Ready time: 30 minutes

Ingredients:
- 1.5 pounds of beef sirloin, cut into 1-inch cubes
- 1 red bell pepper, cut into chunks
- 1 green bell pepper, cut into chunks
- 1 red onion, cut into chunks
- 2 tablespoons of olive oil
- 2 tablespoons of lemon juice
- 2 cloves of garlic, minced
- 1 teaspoon of dried oregano
- Salt and black pepper to taste
For the Tzatziki Sauce:
- 1 cup of Greek yogurt

- 1 cucumber, grated and squeezed to remove excess moisture
- 2 cloves of garlic, minced
- 1 tablespoon of lemon juice
- 1 tablespoon of fresh dill, chopped
- Salt and black pepper to taste

Instructions:
1. In a bowl, combine the olive oil, lemon juice, minced garlic, dried oregano, salt, and black pepper. Mix well to create a marinade.
2. Add the beef cubes to the marinade and toss to coat evenly. Allow the beef to marinate for at least 15 minutes, or up to 2 hours for more flavor.
3. While the beef is marinating, prepare the tzatziki sauce. In a separate bowl, combine the Greek yogurt, grated cucumber, minced garlic, lemon juice, chopped dill, salt, and black pepper. Stir well to combine. Refrigerate until ready to serve.
4. Preheat your grill to medium-high heat.
5. Thread the marinated beef cubes onto skewers, alternating with chunks of red and green bell peppers, and red onion.
6. Place the kebabs on the preheated grill and cook for about 10-12 minutes, turning occasionally, until the beef is cooked to your desired level of doneness.
7. Remove the kebabs from the grill and let them rest for a few minutes.
8. Serve the beef kebabs with the tzatziki sauce on the side. Enjoy!

Nutrition information:
- Calories: 350
- Fat: 18g
- Carbohydrates: 10g
- Protein: 35g
- Fiber: 2g

55. Baked Salmon with Garlic and Herbs

Baked Salmon with Garlic and Herbs is a delicious and healthy dish that is perfect for any occasion. The combination of fresh salmon, aromatic garlic, and flavorful herbs creates a mouthwatering meal that is sure to impress your family and friends. This recipe is easy to make and requires minimal preparation time, making it a great option for busy weeknights or special gatherings.

Serving: 4 servings

Preparation time: 10 minutes

Ready time: 25 minutes

Ingredients:

- 4 salmon fillets (about 6 ounces each)
- 4 cloves of garlic, minced
- 2 tablespoons fresh parsley, chopped
- 1 tablespoon fresh dill, chopped
- 1 tablespoon fresh thyme leaves
- 2 tablespoons olive oil
- Salt and pepper to taste
- Lemon wedges, for Serving:

Instructions:

1. Preheat your oven to 400°F (200°C). Line a baking sheet with parchment paper or lightly grease it with olive oil.
2. In a small bowl, combine the minced garlic, chopped parsley, dill, thyme, olive oil, salt, and pepper. Mix well to create a flavorful herb mixture.
3. Place the salmon fillets on the prepared baking sheet, skin side down. Spread the herb mixture evenly over the top of each fillet, pressing it gently to adhere.
4. Bake the salmon in the preheated oven for about 15-20 minutes, or until it flakes easily with a fork. The cooking time may vary depending on the thickness of the fillets, so keep an eye on them to avoid overcooking.
5. Once the salmon is cooked, remove it from the oven and let it rest for a few minutes before serving. This will allow the flavors to meld together and the fish to become even more tender.
6. Serve the Baked Salmon with Garlic and Herbs hot, garnished with lemon wedges for an extra burst of freshness.

Nutrition information (per serving):

- Calories: 350
- Fat: 20g
- Protein: 35g
- Carbohydrates: 2g
- Fiber: 0g

- Sugar: 0g
- Sodium: 150mg
Note: The nutrition information provided is an estimate and may vary depending on the specific Ingredients used.

56. Chicken Teriyaki

Chicken Teriyaki is a popular Japanese dish that is loved for its sweet and savory flavors. This dish features tender chicken pieces glazed with a delicious teriyaki sauce, making it a perfect choice for a quick and flavorful meal. With a few simple Ingredients and easy steps, you can recreate this classic dish in the comfort of your own kitchen.
Serving: 4 servings
Preparation time: 10 minutes
Ready time: 30 minutes

Ingredients:
- 4 boneless, skinless chicken breasts
- 1/2 cup soy sauce
- 1/4 cup mirin (Japanese sweet rice wine)
- 1/4 cup sake (Japanese rice wine)
- 2 tablespoons brown sugar
- 2 tablespoons honey
- 2 cloves garlic, minced
- 1 teaspoon grated ginger
- 1 tablespoon vegetable oil
- 1 tablespoon cornstarch
- 2 tablespoons water
- Sesame seeds, for garnish (optional)
- Sliced green onions, for garnish (optional)

Instructions:
1. In a bowl, combine soy sauce, mirin, sake, brown sugar, honey, minced garlic, and grated ginger. Stir well until the sugar is dissolved and the mixture is well combined. This will be your teriyaki sauce.
2. Slice the chicken breasts into thin strips or bite-sized pieces.

3. Heat vegetable oil in a large skillet or wok over medium-high heat. Add the chicken pieces and cook until they are browned and cooked through, about 5-6 minutes.

4. Reduce the heat to medium and pour the teriyaki sauce over the chicken. Stir well to coat the chicken evenly with the sauce.

5. In a small bowl, mix cornstarch and water to make a slurry. Add the slurry to the skillet and stir well. Cook for an additional 2-3 minutes, or until the sauce has thickened.

6. Remove the skillet from heat and let the chicken teriyaki rest for a few minutes.

7. Serve the chicken teriyaki over steamed rice or noodles. Garnish with sesame seeds and sliced green onions, if desired.

Nutrition information per Serving: - Calories: 320
- Fat: 6g
- Carbohydrates: 25g
- Protein: 40g
- Fiber: 1g
- Sugar: 18g
- Sodium: 1200mg

Note: Nutrition information may vary depending on the specific Ingredients and brands used.

57. Irish Brown Bread

Irish Brown Bread is a traditional Irish bread that is hearty, dense, and full of flavor. Made with whole wheat flour and buttermilk, this bread is perfect for breakfast or as a side dish for soups and stews. It is easy to make and requires minimal Ingredients, making it a staple in Irish households.

Serving:
This recipe makes one loaf of Irish Brown Bread, which serves about 8 people.

Preparation time:
Preparation time for this bread is approximately 15 minutes.

Ready time:
The bread will be ready to serve in about 1 hour and 30 minutes, including baking time.

Ingredients:
- 2 cups whole wheat flour
- 1 cup all-purpose flour
- 1 teaspoon baking soda
- 1 teaspoon salt
- 2 tablespoons butter, cold and cubed
- 1 3/4 cups buttermilk

Instructions:
1. Preheat your oven to 400°F (200°C). Grease a baking sheet or line it with parchment paper.
2. In a large mixing bowl, combine the whole wheat flour, all-purpose flour, baking soda, and salt.
3. Add the cold, cubed butter to the flour mixture. Use your fingertips to rub the butter into the flour until it resembles coarse crumbs.
4. Make a well in the center of the flour mixture and pour in the buttermilk. Stir with a wooden spoon or your hands until the dough comes together.
5. Turn the dough out onto a lightly floured surface and knead it gently for about 1 minute, until it becomes smooth.
6. Shape the dough into a round loaf and place it on the prepared baking sheet. Use a sharp knife to score a deep cross on the top of the loaf.
7. Bake the bread in the preheated oven for 40-45 minutes, or until it is golden brown and sounds hollow when tapped on the bottom.
8. Remove the bread from the oven and let it cool on a wire rack before slicing and serving.

Nutrition information:
- Serving size: 1 slice (1/8 of the loaf)
- Calories: 180
- Total fat: 3g
- Saturated fat: 1.5g
- Cholesterol: 8mg
- Sodium: 400mg
- Total carbohydrates: 32g
- Dietary fiber: 4g
- Sugars: 2g
- Protein: 6g

Note: Nutrition information may vary depending on the specific brands of Ingredients used.

58. Lamb Chops with Rosemary

Lamb chops with rosemary is a classic dish that combines the tender and juicy flavors of lamb with the aromatic and earthy notes of rosemary. This recipe is perfect for a special occasion or a fancy dinner at home. The combination of these two Ingredients creates a mouthwatering dish that will impress your guests and leave them wanting more.
Serving: 4 servings
Preparation time: 10 minutes
Ready time: 25 minutes

Ingredients:
- 8 lamb chops
- 2 tablespoons olive oil
- 4 cloves of garlic, minced
- 2 tablespoons fresh rosemary, chopped
- Salt and pepper to taste

Instructions:
1. Preheat your grill or stovetop grill pan to medium-high heat.
2. In a small bowl, mix together the olive oil, minced garlic, chopped rosemary, salt, and pepper.
3. Rub the mixture all over the lamb chops, making sure to coat them evenly.
4. Place the lamb chops on the grill and cook for about 4-5 minutes per side for medium-rare, or adjust the cooking time according to your desired level of doneness.
5. Remove the lamb chops from the grill and let them rest for a few minutes before serving.
6. Serve the lamb chops with your favorite side dishes, such as roasted potatoes or a fresh salad.

Nutrition information:
- Calories: 350
- Fat: 25g

- Protein: 30g
- Carbohydrates: 1g
- Fiber: 0g
- Sugar: 0g
- Sodium: 100mg

Note: Nutrition information may vary depending on the specific Ingredients and quantities used.

59. Grilled Shrimp with Mango Salsa

Grilled Shrimp with Mango Salsa is a delicious and refreshing dish that combines the succulent flavors of grilled shrimp with the tropical sweetness of mango salsa. This dish is perfect for a summer barbecue or a light and healthy dinner option. The combination of juicy shrimp and tangy salsa will leave your taste buds craving for more.

Serving: 4 servings
Preparation time: 15 minutes
Ready time: 25 minutes

Ingredients:
- 1 pound of large shrimp, peeled and deveined
- 2 ripe mangoes, peeled and diced
- 1 small red onion, finely chopped
- 1 jalapeno pepper, seeded and minced
- 1/4 cup of fresh cilantro, chopped
- Juice of 1 lime
- Salt and pepper to taste
- Olive oil for grilling

Instructions:
1. Preheat your grill to medium-high heat.
2. In a medium bowl, combine the diced mangoes, red onion, jalapeno pepper, cilantro, lime juice, salt, and pepper. Mix well to combine and set aside to let the flavors meld together.
3. Thread the shrimp onto skewers, making sure to leave a little space between each shrimp.
4. Brush the shrimp with olive oil and season with salt and pepper.

5. Place the shrimp skewers on the preheated grill and cook for about 2-3 minutes per side, or until the shrimp are pink and opaque.
6. Remove the shrimp from the grill and let them rest for a few minutes.
7. Serve the grilled shrimp with a generous spoonful of mango salsa on top.
8. Enjoy!

Nutrition information per Serving: - Calories: 220
- Fat: 3g
- Carbohydrates: 20g
- Protein: 28g
- Fiber: 3g

60. Chicken Shawarma

Chicken Shawarma is a popular Middle Eastern dish that is loved for its flavorful and tender chicken. This dish is made by marinating chicken in a blend of aromatic spices and then grilling it to perfection. The result is a juicy and delicious chicken that is perfect for stuffing into pita bread or serving with rice and salad. With its bold flavors and easy preparation, Chicken Shawarma is sure to become a favorite in your household.
Serving: 4 servings
Preparation time: 15 minutes
Ready time: 1 hour 15 minutes

Ingredients:
- 1.5 pounds boneless, skinless chicken thighs
- 1/4 cup olive oil
- 4 cloves garlic, minced
- 2 tablespoons lemon juice
- 1 tablespoon ground cumin
- 1 tablespoon ground paprika
- 1 teaspoon ground coriander
- 1 teaspoon ground turmeric
- 1/2 teaspoon ground cinnamon
- 1/2 teaspoon ground cayenne pepper (optional, for heat)
- Salt and black pepper to taste

- Pita bread, for Serving: - Toppings such as sliced tomatoes, cucumbers, onions, and tahini sauce (optional)

Instructions:
1. In a large bowl, combine the olive oil, minced garlic, lemon juice, cumin, paprika, coriander, turmeric, cinnamon, cayenne pepper (if using), salt, and black pepper. Mix well to create a marinade.
2. Add the chicken thighs to the marinade and toss to coat them evenly. Cover the bowl with plastic wrap and refrigerate for at least 1 hour, allowing the flavors to meld together.
3. Preheat your grill or grill pan over medium-high heat. Remove the chicken from the marinade and shake off any excess.
4. Grill the chicken thighs for about 6-8 minutes per side, or until they are cooked through and have nice grill marks. The internal temperature should reach 165°F (74°C).
5. Once cooked, transfer the chicken to a cutting board and let it rest for a few minutes. Then, thinly slice the chicken into strips.
6. Serve the Chicken Shawarma in warm pita bread, along with your choice of toppings such as sliced tomatoes, cucumbers, onions, and tahini sauce.
7. Enjoy your homemade Chicken Shawarma!

Nutrition information per Serving: - Calories: 350
- Fat: 18g
- Carbohydrates: 10g
- Protein: 35g
- Fiber: 2g

61. Irish Potato Soup

Irish Potato Soup is a hearty and comforting dish that is perfect for those chilly days. Made with simple Ingredients, this soup is packed with flavor and will warm you up from the inside out. Whether you're Irish or not, this soup is sure to become a favorite in your household.
Serving: 4 servings
Preparation time: 15 minutes
Ready time: 45 minutes

Ingredients:
- 4 large potatoes, peeled and diced
- 1 onion, chopped
- 2 cloves of garlic, minced
- 4 cups vegetable or chicken broth
- 1 cup milk
- 1/2 cup heavy cream
- 2 tablespoons butter
- Salt and pepper to taste
- Fresh chives or parsley for garnish (optional)

Instructions:
1. In a large pot, melt the butter over medium heat. Add the chopped onion and minced garlic, and sauté until they become translucent and fragrant.
2. Add the diced potatoes to the pot and stir well to coat them with the butter and onion mixture. Cook for about 5 minutes, stirring occasionally.
3. Pour in the vegetable or chicken broth, and bring the mixture to a boil. Reduce the heat to low, cover the pot, and let it simmer for about 30 minutes, or until the potatoes are tender.
4. Using an immersion blender or a regular blender, puree the soup until smooth and creamy. If using a regular blender, be sure to blend in batches and exercise caution as the soup will be hot.
5. Return the soup to the pot and stir in the milk and heavy cream. Season with salt and pepper to taste. Heat the soup over low heat until warmed through, but do not let it boil.
6. Ladle the Irish Potato Soup into bowls and garnish with fresh chives or parsley, if desired. Serve hot and enjoy!

Nutrition information per Serving: - Calories: 300
- Fat: 15g
- Carbohydrates: 35g
- Protein: 6g
- Fiber: 4g
- Sodium: 800mg
Note: Nutrition information may vary depending on the specific Ingredients and brands used.

62. Beef and Black Bean Stir-Fry

Beef and Black Bean Stir-Fry is a delicious and nutritious dish that combines tender beef, crisp vegetables, and flavorful black beans. This stir-fry is quick and easy to make, making it a perfect option for a busy weeknight dinner. The combination of savory flavors and textures will surely satisfy your taste buds.

Serving: 4 servings
Preparation time: 15 minutes
Ready time: 25 minutes

Ingredients:
- 1 pound beef sirloin, thinly sliced
- 2 tablespoons vegetable oil
- 3 cloves garlic, minced
- 1 red bell pepper, sliced
- 1 green bell pepper, sliced
- 1 onion, sliced
- 1 cup black beans, rinsed and drained
- 2 tablespoons soy sauce
- 1 tablespoon oyster sauce
- 1 teaspoon cornstarch
- 1/2 cup beef broth
- Salt and pepper to taste
- Cooked rice or noodles, for Serving:

Instructions:
1. In a small bowl, whisk together soy sauce, oyster sauce, cornstarch, and beef broth. Set aside.
2. Heat vegetable oil in a large skillet or wok over medium-high heat.
3. Add minced garlic and sauté for about 1 minute until fragrant.
4. Add beef slices to the skillet and stir-fry for 2-3 minutes until browned. Remove beef from the skillet and set aside.
5. In the same skillet, add sliced bell peppers and onion. Stir-fry for 3-4 minutes until vegetables are crisp-tender.
6. Return the beef to the skillet and add black beans. Stir-fry for another 2 minutes.
7. Pour the sauce mixture over the beef and vegetables. Stir well to coat everything evenly.

8. Cook for an additional 2-3 minutes until the sauce thickens and coats the stir-fry.
9. Season with salt and pepper to taste.
10. Serve the Beef and Black Bean Stir-Fry over cooked rice or noodles.

Nutrition information:
- Calories: 320
- Fat: 12g
- Carbohydrates: 20g
- Protein: 30g
- Fiber: 5g
- Sugar: 4g
- Sodium: 800mg

63. Cajun Shrimp Pasta

Cajun Shrimp Pasta is a delicious and flavorful dish that combines succulent shrimp with a spicy Cajun seasoning and creamy pasta. This dish is perfect for those who love a little heat in their meals and can be easily prepared in no time. Whether you're cooking for a special occasion or simply craving a comforting meal, this Cajun Shrimp Pasta will surely satisfy your taste buds.
Serving: 4 servings
Preparation time: 10 minutes
Ready time: 25 minutes

Ingredients:
- 8 ounces linguine or spaghetti
- 1 pound large shrimp, peeled and deveined
- 2 tablespoons Cajun seasoning
- 2 tablespoons olive oil
- 1 red bell pepper, thinly sliced
- 1 green bell pepper, thinly sliced
- 1 small onion, thinly sliced
- 3 cloves garlic, minced
- 1 cup heavy cream
- 1/2 cup chicken broth
- 1/2 teaspoon salt

- 1/4 teaspoon black pepper
- Fresh parsley, chopped (for garnish)

Instructions:
1. Cook the linguine or spaghetti according to the package instructions until al dente. Drain and set aside.
2. In a medium bowl, toss the shrimp with the Cajun seasoning until evenly coated.
3. Heat the olive oil in a large skillet over medium-high heat. Add the seasoned shrimp and cook for 2-3 minutes per side until pink and cooked through. Remove the shrimp from the skillet and set aside.
4. In the same skillet, add the sliced bell peppers, onion, and minced garlic. Sauté for 5 minutes until the vegetables are tender.
5. Reduce the heat to medium and pour in the heavy cream and chicken broth. Stir well to combine.
6. Season the sauce with salt and black pepper. Let it simmer for 5 minutes until slightly thickened.
7. Add the cooked linguine or spaghetti to the skillet and toss to coat the pasta with the creamy sauce.
8. Return the cooked shrimp to the skillet and gently stir to combine.
9. Cook for an additional 2-3 minutes until everything is heated through.
10. Serve the Cajun Shrimp Pasta hot, garnished with fresh parsley.

Nutrition information:
- Calories: 480
- Fat: 26g
- Carbohydrates: 36g
- Protein: 28g
- Fiber: 3g

64. Guinness Beef Stew

Guinness Beef Stew is a hearty and flavorful dish that combines tender beef, vegetables, and the rich taste of Guinness beer. This traditional Irish stew is perfect for cold winter nights or any time you're craving a comforting meal. The slow cooking process allows the flavors to meld together, resulting in a delicious and satisfying dish.
Serving: 4 servings

Preparation time: 20 minutes
Ready time: 2 hours 30 minutes

Ingredients:
- 1.5 pounds beef stew meat, cut into bite-sized pieces
- 2 tablespoons all-purpose flour
- Salt and pepper, to taste
- 2 tablespoons vegetable oil
- 1 onion, diced
- 3 cloves garlic, minced
- 2 carrots, peeled and sliced
- 2 celery stalks, sliced
- 2 potatoes, peeled and diced
- 1 cup Guinness beer
- 2 cups beef broth
- 2 tablespoons tomato paste
- 1 tablespoon Worcestershire sauce
- 1 bay leaf
- Fresh parsley, for garnish (optional)

Instructions:
1. In a large bowl, combine the flour, salt, and pepper. Toss the beef stew meat in the flour mixture until evenly coated.
2. Heat the vegetable oil in a large pot or Dutch oven over medium-high heat. Add the beef stew meat and cook until browned on all sides. Remove the meat from the pot and set aside.
3. In the same pot, add the diced onion and minced garlic. Sauté until the onion becomes translucent and fragrant.
4. Add the carrots, celery, and potatoes to the pot. Cook for a few minutes until the vegetables start to soften.
5. Return the browned beef stew meat to the pot. Pour in the Guinness beer, beef broth, tomato paste, Worcestershire sauce, and add the bay leaf.
6. Bring the stew to a boil, then reduce the heat to low. Cover the pot and simmer for about 2 hours, or until the beef is tender and the flavors have melded together.
7. Remove the bay leaf from the stew before serving. Garnish with fresh parsley, if desired.
8. Serve the Guinness Beef Stew hot with crusty bread or over mashed potatoes.

Nutrition information:
- Calories: 380
- Fat: 12g
- Carbohydrates: 28g
- Protein: 35g
- Fiber: 4g
- Sugar: 4g
- Sodium: 800mg

65. Chicken Enchiladas

Chicken Enchiladas are a delicious and flavorful Mexican dish that is perfect for a family dinner or a gathering with friends. These enchiladas are filled with tender chicken, cheese, and a savory sauce, all wrapped in soft tortillas. With a little bit of spice and a whole lot of flavor, this dish is sure to be a hit!

Serving: 4 servings
Preparation time: 20 minutes
Ready time: 40 minutes

Ingredients:
- 2 cups cooked chicken, shredded
- 1 cup shredded cheddar cheese
- 1 cup shredded Monterey Jack cheese
- 1 small onion, diced
- 1 can (4 ounces) diced green chilies
- 1 can (10 ounces) red enchilada sauce
- 1/2 cup sour cream
- 1/4 cup chopped fresh cilantro
- 8 small flour tortillas
- Salt and pepper to taste

Instructions:
1. Preheat your oven to 375°F (190°C). Grease a 9x13-inch baking dish and set aside.
2. In a large bowl, combine the shredded chicken, cheddar cheese, Monterey Jack cheese, diced onion, diced green chilies, sour cream, and

chopped cilantro. Mix well until all the Ingredients are evenly combined. Season with salt and pepper to taste.

3. Warm the flour tortillas in the microwave for about 30 seconds to make them more pliable. This will make it easier to roll the enchiladas.

4. Spoon about 1/4 cup of the chicken mixture onto each tortilla and roll it up tightly. Place the rolled enchiladas seam-side down in the prepared baking dish.

5. Pour the red enchilada sauce evenly over the enchiladas, making sure to cover them completely. Sprinkle any remaining cheese on top.

6. Cover the baking dish with aluminum foil and bake in the preheated oven for 25 minutes. Then, remove the foil and bake for an additional 10 minutes, or until the cheese is melted and bubbly.

7. Once cooked, remove the enchiladas from the oven and let them cool for a few minutes before serving. Garnish with additional chopped cilantro, if desired.

Nutrition information:
- Calories: 450
- Fat: 22g
- Carbohydrates: 32g
- Protein: 30g
- Fiber: 3g
- Sugar: 4g
- Sodium: 800mg
Note: Nutrition information may vary depending on the specific brands and quantities of Ingredients used.

66. Smoked Salmon and Avocado Salad

This Smoked Salmon and Avocado Salad is a refreshing and nutritious dish that combines the rich flavors of smoked salmon and creamy avocado. Packed with healthy fats and protein, this salad is perfect for a light lunch or a satisfying dinner. The combination of fresh Ingredients and a tangy dressing makes this salad a crowd-pleaser.
Serving: 2 servings
Preparation time: 15 minutes
Ready time: 15 minutes

Ingredients:
- 4 cups mixed salad greens
- 8 ounces smoked salmon, sliced
- 1 ripe avocado, sliced
- 1/2 red onion, thinly sliced
- 1/4 cup cherry tomatoes, halved
- 2 tablespoons capers
- 1/4 cup fresh dill, chopped
- 2 tablespoons extra virgin olive oil
- 1 tablespoon lemon juice
- Salt and pepper to taste

Instructions:
1. In a large salad bowl, combine the mixed salad greens, smoked salmon, avocado, red onion, cherry tomatoes, capers, and fresh dill.
2. In a small bowl, whisk together the extra virgin olive oil, lemon juice, salt, and pepper to make the dressing.
3. Drizzle the dressing over the salad and gently toss to combine all the Ingredients.
4. Divide the salad into two plates or bowls.
5. Serve immediately and enjoy!

Nutrition information per Serving: - Calories: 350
- Fat: 25g
- Protein: 20g
- Carbohydrates: 10g
- Fiber: 6g
- Sugar: 2g
- Sodium: 600mg

Note: Nutrition information may vary depending on the specific brands and quantities of Ingredients used.

67. Irish Lamb Pie

Irish Lamb Pie is a hearty and comforting dish that is perfect for a cozy dinner. This traditional Irish recipe combines tender lamb, vegetables, and a rich gravy, all topped with a flaky pastry crust. It's a delicious and satisfying meal that will warm you up from the inside out.

Serving: 6 servings
Preparation time: 30 minutes
Ready time: 2 hours

Ingredients:
- 2 pounds lamb shoulder, cut into bite-sized pieces
- 2 tablespoons vegetable oil
- 1 onion, diced
- 2 carrots, diced
- 2 celery stalks, diced
- 3 cloves of garlic, minced
- 2 tablespoons all-purpose flour
- 1 cup beef or vegetable broth
- 1 cup Guinness or other stout beer
- 1 tablespoon Worcestershire sauce
- 1 teaspoon dried thyme
- Salt and pepper to taste
- 1 sheet of puff pastry, thawed
- 1 egg, beaten (for egg wash)

Instructions:
1. Preheat your oven to 375°F (190°C).
2. In a large oven-safe pot or Dutch oven, heat the vegetable oil over medium-high heat. Add the lamb pieces and brown them on all sides. Remove the lamb from the pot and set it aside.
3. In the same pot, add the diced onion, carrots, celery, and minced garlic. Sauté until the vegetables are softened, about 5 minutes.
4. Sprinkle the flour over the vegetables and stir well to coat. Cook for an additional 2 minutes to cook off the raw flour taste.
5. Slowly pour in the beef or vegetable broth and Guinness beer, stirring constantly to avoid any lumps. Add the Worcestershire sauce, dried thyme, salt, and pepper. Bring the mixture to a simmer.
6. Return the browned lamb to the pot and stir to combine. Cover the pot with a lid and transfer it to the preheated oven.
7. Bake for 1.5 to 2 hours, or until the lamb is tender and the flavors have melded together.
8. While the lamb is cooking, roll out the puff pastry sheet on a lightly floured surface. Cut it into a shape that will fit over the top of your pot.
9. Once the lamb is done, remove the pot from the oven and increase the oven temperature to 400°F (200°C).

10. Carefully place the puff pastry over the top of the pot, sealing the edges. Brush the pastry with the beaten egg to give it a golden shine.
11. Return the pot to the oven and bake for an additional 20-25 minutes, or until the pastry is puffed and golden.
12. Remove from the oven and let it cool for a few minutes before serving.

Nutrition information per Serving: - Calories: 450
- Fat: 25g
- Carbohydrates: 25g
- Protein: 30g
- Fiber: 3g
- Sugar: 3g
- Sodium: 500mg
Note: Nutrition information may vary depending on the specific Ingredients and brands used.

68. Seared Scallops with Lemon Butter Sauce

Seared Scallops with Lemon Butter Sauce is a delightful seafood dish that combines the succulent flavors of perfectly seared scallops with a tangy and buttery lemon sauce. This dish is not only elegant and impressive, but it is also incredibly easy to make. Whether you are hosting a dinner party or simply craving a gourmet meal at home, this recipe is sure to satisfy your taste buds.
Serving: 4 servings
Preparation time: 10 minutes
Ready time: 20 minutes

Ingredients:
- 1 pound fresh scallops
- Salt and pepper, to taste
- 2 tablespoons olive oil
- 4 tablespoons unsalted butter
- 2 cloves garlic, minced
- 1/4 cup fresh lemon juice
- 1 tablespoon lemon zest
- 2 tablespoons fresh parsley, chopped

Instructions:
1. Start by patting the scallops dry with a paper towel. Season them generously with salt and pepper on both sides.
2. Heat the olive oil in a large skillet over medium-high heat. Once the oil is hot, carefully add the scallops to the skillet, making sure not to overcrowd them. Cook for about 2-3 minutes on each side until they develop a golden brown crust. Remove the scallops from the skillet and set them aside.
3. In the same skillet, melt the butter over medium heat. Add the minced garlic and cook for about 1 minute until fragrant.
4. Stir in the lemon juice and lemon zest, scraping any browned bits from the bottom of the skillet. Cook for an additional 2 minutes until the sauce slightly thickens.
5. Return the seared scallops to the skillet and toss them gently in the lemon butter sauce. Cook for another minute to heat the scallops through.
6. Sprinkle the chopped parsley over the scallops and sauce, giving it a final toss.
7. Remove from heat and serve the seared scallops with lemon butter sauce immediately.

Nutrition information:
- Calories: 250
- Fat: 16g
- Carbohydrates: 4g
- Protein: 22g
- Fiber: 0g
- Sugar: 1g
- Sodium: 400mg

Note: The nutrition information provided is an estimate and may vary depending on the specific Ingredients used.

69. Beef Tamales

Beef Tamales are a traditional Mexican dish that is loved for its flavorful filling and tender corn masa dough. These delicious parcels are perfect for a hearty meal or a special occasion. The combination of seasoned beef and masa creates a mouthwatering dish that will leave you craving for more. Follow this recipe to make your own homemade Beef Tamales that will surely impress your family and friends.

Serving: 8 tamales

Preparation time: 1 hour

Ready time: 3 hours

Ingredients:
- 1 pound beef chuck roast, trimmed and cut into small cubes
- 1 tablespoon vegetable oil
- 1 onion, finely chopped
- 2 cloves garlic, minced
- 1 teaspoon ground cumin
- 1 teaspoon chili powder
- 1 teaspoon dried oregano
- Salt and pepper to taste
- 2 cups masa harina (corn flour)
- 1 ½ cups beef broth
- 8 dried corn husks, soaked in warm water for 30 minutes

Instructions:
1. In a large skillet, heat the vegetable oil over medium heat. Add the chopped onion and minced garlic, and sauté until they become translucent.
2. Add the beef cubes to the skillet and cook until browned on all sides. Season with cumin, chili powder, dried oregano, salt, and pepper. Stir well to coat the beef with the spices.
3. Pour in 1 cup of beef broth and bring to a simmer. Reduce the heat to low, cover the skillet, and let the beef cook for about 2 hours or until it becomes tender and easily shreds with a fork. Stir occasionally and add more broth if needed.
4. While the beef is cooking, prepare the corn masa dough. In a large mixing bowl, combine the masa harina with the remaining ½ cup of beef broth. Mix well until a soft dough forms. If the dough feels too dry, add a little more broth.
5. Drain the soaked corn husks and pat them dry. Take one corn husk and spread about 2 tablespoons of the masa dough onto the center, leaving a border around the edges.
6. Spoon a generous amount of the cooked beef onto the masa dough. Fold the sides of the corn husk towards the center, enclosing the filling,

and then fold the bottom of the husk up. Secure the tamale by tying it with a strip of soaked corn husk or kitchen twine.

7. Repeat the process with the remaining corn husks, masa dough, and beef filling until all the Ingredients are used.

8. Place a steamer basket in a large pot and fill it with water, making sure the water level is below the basket. Arrange the tamales upright in the steamer basket, with the open ends facing up.

9. Cover the pot with a lid and steam the tamales over medium heat for about 1 hour and 30 minutes, or until the masa dough is firm and easily pulls away from the corn husks.

10. Remove the tamales from the steamer and let them cool for a few minutes before serving. Unwrap the corn husks and enjoy the delicious Beef Tamales.

Nutrition information per Serving: - Calories: 320
- Fat: 12g
- Carbohydrates: 35g
- Protein: 18g
- Fiber: 4g

70. Lemon Garlic Roast Chicken

Lemon Garlic Roast Chicken is a classic Mediterranean dish - combining garlic, lemon and chicken for an easy dinner recipe that is both flavorful and comforting.

Serving: 4
Preparation time: 10 min
Ready time: 1 hr

Ingredients:
- 4-5 cloves of garlic
- 2 lemons
- 2 tablespoons of olive oil
- 1 tablespoon of thyme
- Salt and black pepper, to taste
- 2.5 pound whole chicken

Instructions:

1. Preheat oven to 375°F.
2. Peel garlic cloves and finely mince. Cut lemons in half and juice one half.
3. In a small bowl, mix garlic, lemon juice, olive oil, thyme, salt and pepper.
4. Pat chicken dry and place onto a baking sheet. Rub the garlic lemon mix all over the chicken.
5. Place chicken in oven and bake for approximately 1 hour, depending on size.
6. Halfway through cooking, baste chicken with leftover mixture and turn over once when done.
7. Slice other half of lemon and squeeze slices over cooked chicken.

Nutrition information:
Calories: 429;
Fat: 24g;
Saturated fat: 6g;
Carbohydrates: 9g;
Protein: 42g;
Cholesterol: 155mg;
Sodium: 484mg.

71. Irish Cabbage Rolls

Irish Cabbage Rolls are a flavorful, comforting meal that you can make with just a few Ingredients. This simple dish combines nutritious cabbage and ground beef cooked in an easy-to-prepare sauce that you can serve with your favorite starch.
Serving: Serves 6
Preparation time: 10 minutes
Ready time: 40 minutes

Ingredients:
- 2 tablespoons olive oil
- 1 small onion, diced
- 1 lb ground beef
- 1 tablespoon garlic, minced
- 1/2 teaspoon cumin

- 2 tablespoons tomato paste
- 2 cups cooked rice
- 1/2 head cabbage, shredded
- 4 cups beef stock
- Salt and pepper, to taste

Instructions:
1. Heat the olive oil in a large skillet over medium heat. Add the diced onion and cook until softened, about 5 minutes.
2. Add in the ground beef and cook until browned, about 8 minutes. Stir in the garlic, cumin, and tomato paste.
3. Add the cooked rice, shredded cabbage, and beef stock. Season with salt and pepper. Bring to a boil then reduce the heat to a simmer.
4. Cover and simmer for 25 minutes, stirring occasionally. The cabbage should be softened and the liquid should be reduced.
5. Serve the Irish Cabbage Rolls with your favorite starch.

Nutrition information:
Calories: 241; Fat: 10g; Protein: 16g;Carbohydrates: 19g; Sodium: 471mg; Fiber: 2.3g.

72. Shrimp Stir-Fry with Vegetables

Shrimp Stir-Fry with Vegetables is a delicious and healthy dish that combines succulent shrimp with a medley of colorful vegetables. This quick and easy recipe is perfect for a weeknight dinner when you want something flavorful and nutritious on the table in no time. The combination of tender shrimp, crisp vegetables, and a savory sauce makes this stir-fry a crowd-pleaser.
Serving: 4 servings
Preparation time: 15 minutes
Ready time: 20 minutes

Ingredients:
- 1 pound of shrimp, peeled and deveined
- 2 tablespoons of vegetable oil
- 1 red bell pepper, sliced
- 1 yellow bell pepper, sliced

- 1 small onion, sliced
- 2 cloves of garlic, minced
- 1 cup of broccoli florets
- 1 cup of snap peas
- 1 cup of sliced carrots
- 1/4 cup of soy sauce
- 2 tablespoons of oyster sauce
- 1 tablespoon of cornstarch
- 1/2 cup of chicken or vegetable broth
- Salt and pepper to taste
- Optional: sesame seeds and green onions for garnish

Instructions:
1. In a small bowl, whisk together the soy sauce, oyster sauce, cornstarch, and broth. Set aside.
2. Heat one tablespoon of vegetable oil in a large skillet or wok over medium-high heat.
3. Add the shrimp to the skillet and cook for 2-3 minutes on each side until pink and cooked through. Remove the shrimp from the skillet and set aside.
4. In the same skillet, add the remaining tablespoon of vegetable oil and sauté the garlic, onion, and bell peppers for 2-3 minutes until slightly softened.
5. Add the broccoli, snap peas, and carrots to the skillet and cook for an additional 3-4 minutes until the vegetables are crisp-tender.
6. Return the shrimp to the skillet and pour the sauce mixture over the shrimp and vegetables. Stir well to coat everything evenly.
7. Cook for another 2-3 minutes until the sauce has thickened and the shrimp and vegetables are fully coated.
8. Season with salt and pepper to taste.
9. Remove from heat and garnish with sesame seeds and green onions if desired.
10. Serve the shrimp stir-fry with vegetables over steamed rice or noodles.

Nutrition information:
- Calories: 250
- Fat: 8g
- Carbohydrates: 20g
- Protein: 25g

- Fiber: 4g
- Sugar: 8g
- Sodium: 800mg

73. Chicken Korma

Chicken Korma is a delicious and aromatic Indian dish that is known for its rich and creamy sauce. Made with tender chicken pieces cooked in a flavorful blend of spices, yogurt, and cream, this dish is perfect for those who enjoy a mild yet flavorful curry. Serve it with steamed rice or naan bread for a complete and satisfying meal.
Serving: 4 servings
Preparation time: 15 minutes
Ready time: 45 minutes

Ingredients:
- 500 grams boneless chicken, cut into bite-sized pieces
- 2 tablespoons vegetable oil
- 1 large onion, finely chopped
- 2 cloves of garlic, minced
- 1-inch piece of ginger, grated
- 2 green chilies, slit lengthwise (optional)
- 1 teaspoon ground cumin
- 1 teaspoon ground coriander
- 1/2 teaspoon turmeric powder
- 1/2 teaspoon red chili powder (adjust to taste)
- 1/2 cup plain yogurt, whisked
- 1/2 cup heavy cream
- Salt to taste
- Fresh cilantro leaves, for garnish

Instructions:
1. Heat the vegetable oil in a large pan or skillet over medium heat. Add the chopped onions and sauté until they turn golden brown.
2. Add the minced garlic, grated ginger, and green chilies (if using) to the pan. Sauté for another minute until fragrant.

3. In a small bowl, mix together the ground cumin, ground coriander, turmeric powder, and red chili powder. Add this spice mixture to the pan and cook for a minute, stirring constantly.

4. Add the chicken pieces to the pan and cook until they are lightly browned on all sides.

5. Reduce the heat to low and add the whisked yogurt to the pan. Stir well to combine the yogurt with the spices and coat the chicken evenly.

6. Cover the pan and let the chicken cook in the yogurt mixture for about 20-25 minutes, or until it is cooked through and tender.

7. Stir in the heavy cream and season with salt to taste. Cook for an additional 5 minutes to allow the flavors to meld together.

8. Garnish with fresh cilantro leaves before serving.

Nutrition information:
- Calories: 350 per Serving: - Fat: 20g
- Carbohydrates: 10g
- Protein: 30g
- Fiber: 2g

74. Seafood Gumbo

Seafood Gumbo is a delicious and hearty dish that originates from the southern United States. This flavorful stew is packed with a variety of seafood, vegetables, and spices, creating a perfect balance of flavors. Whether you're a seafood lover or just looking to try something new, this Seafood Gumbo recipe is sure to impress!

Serving: 6 servings
Preparation time: 20 minutes
Ready time: 1 hour 30 minutes

Ingredients:
- 1/2 cup vegetable oil
- 1/2 cup all-purpose flour
- 1 large onion, diced
- 1 green bell pepper, diced
- 2 celery stalks, diced
- 4 cloves of garlic, minced
- 1 can (14.5 oz) diced tomatoes

- 4 cups seafood stock
- 1 bay leaf
- 1 teaspoon dried thyme
- 1 teaspoon dried oregano
- 1/2 teaspoon cayenne pepper (adjust to taste)
- 1 pound shrimp, peeled and deveined
- 1 pound crab meat
- 1 pound fresh or frozen okra, sliced
- Salt and pepper to taste
- Cooked white rice, for Serving: - Chopped green onions, for garnish

Instructions:

1. In a large pot or Dutch oven, heat the vegetable oil over medium heat. Add the flour and stir constantly to make a roux. Cook the roux, stirring frequently, until it turns a dark brown color, similar to the color of chocolate. This process may take about 15-20 minutes, so be patient and keep stirring to prevent burning.

2. Once the roux is dark brown, add the diced onion, bell pepper, celery, and minced garlic to the pot. Cook the vegetables for about 5 minutes, until they start to soften.

3. Add the diced tomatoes, seafood stock, bay leaf, dried thyme, dried oregano, and cayenne pepper to the pot. Stir well to combine all the Ingredients. Bring the mixture to a boil, then reduce the heat to low and let it simmer for about 45 minutes, stirring occasionally.

4. After the gumbo has simmered for 45 minutes, add the shrimp, crab meat, and sliced okra to the pot. Stir gently to incorporate the seafood and vegetables into the stew. Cook for an additional 10-15 minutes, until the shrimp are pink and cooked through.

5. Season the gumbo with salt and pepper to taste. Remove the bay leaf from the pot.

6. Serve the Seafood Gumbo hot over cooked white rice. Garnish with chopped green onions for added freshness and flavor.

Nutrition information:

- Calories: 380
- Fat: 18g
- Carbohydrates: 20g
- Protein: 35g
- Fiber: 4g
- Sodium: 800mg

Note: Nutrition information may vary depending on the specific
Ingredients used.

75. Beef Rendang

Beef Rendang is a traditional Indonesian dish that is rich in flavor and
spices. It is a slow-cooked beef curry that is tender, aromatic, and packed
with a perfect blend of spices. This dish is perfect for those who enjoy a
spicy and flavorful meal.
Serving: 4 servings
Preparation time: 20 minutes
Ready time: 3 hours

Ingredients:
- 1 kg beef, cut into cubes
- 4 tablespoons vegetable oil
- 2 onions, finely chopped
- 4 cloves garlic, minced
- 2 lemongrass stalks, bruised
- 4 kaffir lime leaves
- 2 teaspoons turmeric powder
- 2 teaspoons ground coriander
- 1 teaspoon ground cumin
- 1 teaspoon chili powder (adjust according to your spice preference)
- 400 ml coconut milk
- 1 tablespoon tamarind paste
- Salt, to taste

Instructions:
1. Heat the vegetable oil in a large pot over medium heat. Add the
chopped onions and minced garlic, and sauté until they turn golden
brown.
2. Add the beef cubes to the pot and cook until they are browned on all
sides.
3. Add the bruised lemongrass stalks, kaffir lime leaves, turmeric powder,
ground coriander, ground cumin, and chili powder to the pot. Stir well to
coat the beef with the spices.

4. Pour in the coconut milk and tamarind paste. Stir everything together and bring it to a boil.

5. Once it starts boiling, reduce the heat to low and cover the pot. Let it simmer for about 2-3 hours, or until the beef is tender and the sauce has thickened. Stir occasionally to prevent sticking.

6. Season with salt according to your taste preference.

7. Serve the Beef Rendang hot with steamed rice or roti.

Nutrition information:
- Calories: 450 per Serving: - Fat: 30g
- Carbohydrates: 10g
- Protein: 35g
- Fiber: 2g

76. Baked Cod with Tomato and Olives

This delicious Baked Cod with Tomato and Olives recipe is a simple and healthy dish that is packed full of flavor. It's perfect for busy weeknights, and can be prepped in 5 minutes!
Serving: Serves 4
Preparation Time: 5 minutes
Ready Time: 25 minutes

Ingredients:
• 2 lbs cod fillet
• 2 tablespoons olive oil
• 2 cloves garlic, minced
• 1/2 teaspoon crushed red pepper
• 1 teaspoon dried oregano
• 2 cups grape tomatoes, halved
• 1/2 cup kalamata olives, pitted and halved
• 1/4 cup parsley, minced
• Salt and freshly ground black pepper to taste

Instructions:
1. Preheat oven to 375°F
2. Place cod in a 9x13-inch glass baking dish

3. In a medium bowl, combine olive oil, garlic, red pepper, oregano, tomatoes, olives, and parsley
4. Spread this mixture over the top of the fish
5. Sprinkle with salt and pepper
6. Bake in preheated oven for 20 to 25 minutes, or until fish is cooked through
7. Serve with a side of steamed vegetables and crusty bread

Nutrition information:
Calories: 223, Fat: 6.3g, Cholesterol: 56mg, Sodium: 294mg, Carbohydrates: 5.8g, Protein: 33g

77. Chicken and Vegetable Curry

Chicken and Vegetable Curry is a delicious and flavorful dish that combines tender chicken pieces with a medley of vegetables in a rich and aromatic curry sauce. This dish is perfect for those who love a good balance of protein and veggies in their meals. With its vibrant colors and fragrant spices, this curry is sure to be a hit at your dinner table.
Serving: 4 servings
Preparation time: 15 minutes
Ready time: 45 minutes

Ingredients:
- 1 lb boneless, skinless chicken breasts, cut into bite-sized pieces
- 1 tablespoon vegetable oil
- 1 onion, finely chopped
- 3 cloves of garlic, minced
- 1 tablespoon ginger, grated
- 2 tablespoons curry powder
- 1 teaspoon turmeric powder
- 1 teaspoon cumin powder
- 1 teaspoon coriander powder
- 1 teaspoon paprika
- 1 can (14 oz) coconut milk
- 1 cup chicken broth
- 2 carrots, peeled and sliced
- 1 bell pepper, diced

- 1 zucchini, sliced
- 1 cup frozen peas
- Salt and pepper to taste
- Fresh cilantro, chopped (for garnish)

Instructions:
1. Heat the vegetable oil in a large skillet or pot over medium heat. Add the chopped onion and cook until it becomes translucent, about 5 minutes.
2. Add the minced garlic and grated ginger to the skillet and cook for an additional 1-2 minutes, until fragrant.
3. In a small bowl, combine the curry powder, turmeric powder, cumin powder, coriander powder, and paprika. Stir well to create a spice mixture.
4. Add the chicken pieces to the skillet and sprinkle the spice mixture over them. Cook until the chicken is browned on all sides, about 5-7 minutes.
5. Pour in the coconut milk and chicken broth, stirring well to combine. Bring the mixture to a simmer and let it cook for 10 minutes, allowing the flavors to meld together.
6. Add the sliced carrots, diced bell pepper, and sliced zucchini to the skillet. Cover and cook for an additional 10-15 minutes, or until the vegetables are tender.
7. Stir in the frozen peas and cook for another 2-3 minutes, until they are heated through.
8. Season with salt and pepper to taste. If desired, garnish with fresh cilantro before serving.
9. Serve the Chicken and Vegetable Curry over steamed rice or with naan bread for a complete and satisfying meal.

Nutrition information per Serving: - Calories: 320
- Fat: 15g
- Carbohydrates: 18g
- Protein: 28g
- Fiber: 5g

78. Irish Oatmeal Cookies

Irish Oatmeal Cookies are a delightful treat that combines the wholesome goodness of oats with the sweetness of raisins and a hint of cinnamon. These cookies are perfect for a cozy afternoon snack or as a sweet addition to your morning coffee. They are easy to make and will surely become a favorite in your household.

Serving: Makes approximately 24 cookies
Preparation time: 15 minutes
Ready time: 30 minutes

Ingredients:
- 1 cup unsalted butter, softened
- 1 cup granulated sugar
- 1 cup packed brown sugar
- 2 large eggs
- 1 teaspoon vanilla extract
- 2 cups all-purpose flour
- 1 teaspoon baking soda
- 1 teaspoon ground cinnamon
- 1/2 teaspoon salt
- 3 cups old-fashioned oats
- 1 cup raisins

Instructions:
1. Preheat your oven to 350°F (175°C) and line a baking sheet with parchment paper.
2. In a large mixing bowl, cream together the softened butter, granulated sugar, and brown sugar until light and fluffy.
3. Add the eggs one at a time, beating well after each addition. Stir in the vanilla extract.
4. In a separate bowl, whisk together the flour, baking soda, ground cinnamon, and salt.
5. Gradually add the dry Ingredients to the butter mixture, mixing until just combined.
6. Stir in the oats and raisins until evenly distributed throughout the dough.
7. Drop rounded tablespoonfuls of dough onto the prepared baking sheet, spacing them about 2 inches apart.
8. Bake for 10-12 minutes, or until the edges are golden brown.
9. Allow the cookies to cool on the baking sheet for 5 minutes, then transfer them to a wire rack to cool completely.

Nutrition information per serving (1 cookie):
- Calories: 180
- Total Fat: 8g
- Saturated Fat: 4.5g
- Cholesterol: 30mg
- Sodium: 100mg
- Total Carbohydrate: 26g
- Dietary Fiber: 1g
- Sugars: 15g
- Protein: 2g

Note: Nutrition information may vary depending on the specific Ingredients and brands used.

79. Beef Fajitas

Beef fajitas are a delicious and flavorful Mexican dish that is perfect for a quick and easy weeknight dinner. This recipe combines tender strips of beef with colorful bell peppers and onions, all seasoned with a zesty blend of spices. Serve these beef fajitas with warm tortillas and your favorite toppings for a satisfying and mouthwatering meal.

Serving: 4 servings
Preparation time: 15 minutes
Ready time: 30 minutes

Ingredients:
- 1 pound beef sirloin, thinly sliced
- 2 bell peppers (any color), thinly sliced
- 1 large onion, thinly sliced
- 2 tablespoons vegetable oil
- 2 cloves garlic, minced
- 1 teaspoon chili powder
- 1 teaspoon cumin
- 1/2 teaspoon paprika
- 1/2 teaspoon salt
- 1/4 teaspoon black pepper
- Juice of 1 lime
- 8 small flour tortillas

- Optional toppings: sour cream, guacamole, salsa, shredded cheese

Instructions:
1. In a large bowl, combine the chili powder, cumin, paprika, salt, black pepper, minced garlic, and lime juice. Mix well to create a marinade.
2. Add the thinly sliced beef to the marinade and toss until all the beef is coated. Let it marinate for at least 10 minutes, or up to overnight in the refrigerator for maximum flavor.
3. Heat 1 tablespoon of vegetable oil in a large skillet or grill pan over medium-high heat. Add the marinated beef and cook for 3-4 minutes per side, or until browned and cooked to your desired level of doneness. Remove the beef from the skillet and set aside.
4. In the same skillet, add the remaining tablespoon of vegetable oil and sauté the sliced bell peppers and onions until they are tender and slightly caramelized, about 5-6 minutes.
5. Return the cooked beef to the skillet with the peppers and onions. Stir everything together and cook for an additional 2-3 minutes to allow the flavors to meld.
6. Warm the flour tortillas in a dry skillet or microwave until soft and pliable.
7. To serve, spoon the beef, peppers, and onions onto the warm tortillas. Add your favorite toppings such as sour cream, guacamole, salsa, and shredded cheese.
8. Roll up the tortillas tightly and enjoy your delicious beef fajitas!

Nutrition information (per serving):
- Calories: 380
- Fat: 15g
- Carbohydrates: 32g
- Protein: 28g
- Fiber: 4g
- Sugar: 4g
- Sodium: 550mg

80. Coconut Shrimp with Sweet Chili Sauce

Enjoy a fun and flavorful dish of Coconut Shrimp with Sweet Chili Sauce! This classic combination is an easy way to impress any dinner guest, no matter the occasion.

Serving: 4

Preparation Time: 10 minutes

Ready Time: 30 minutes

Ingredients:
- 1 pound large shrimp, peeled and de-veined
- 1/4 cup all-purpose flour
- 2 cups shredded coconut
- 2 tablespoons olive oil
- 1 teaspoon sea salt
- 1 cup Sweet Chili Sauce

Instructions:
1. Preheat the oven to 375 degrees F.
2. In a shallow bowl, combine the flour and shredded coconut.
3. In another bowl, coat the shrimp in the olive oil and salt.
4. Dip the shrimp into the flour and coconut mixture and place on a parchment lined baking sheet.
5. Bake the shrimp for 10-15 minutes or until golden and cooked through.
6. Place the shrimp onto a serving plate and drizzle with the Sweet Chili Sauce.

Nutrition information: (Per Serving)
Calories: 576

Fat: 25g

Carbohydrates: 75g

Protein: 25g

Sodium: 1164mg

81. Lamb Tagine with Apricots and Almonds

Lamb Tagine with Apricots and Almonds is a delicious and aromatic Moroccan dish that combines tender lamb, sweet apricots, and crunchy almonds. This hearty and flavorful tagine is perfect for a cozy dinner or for entertaining guests. The slow cooking process allows the flavors to meld together, resulting in a dish that is rich and satisfying. Serve this tagine with couscous or warm crusty bread for a complete meal.

Serving: 4 servings

Preparation time: 20 minutes

Ready time: 2 hours 30 minutes

Ingredients:

- 2 pounds lamb shoulder, cut into chunks
- 1 onion, finely chopped
- 3 cloves of garlic, minced
- 1 teaspoon ground cumin
- 1 teaspoon ground coriander
- 1 teaspoon ground cinnamon
- 1 teaspoon paprika
- 1/2 teaspoon ground ginger
- 1/4 teaspoon cayenne pepper (optional, for heat)
- 1 cup dried apricots
- 1/2 cup whole almonds
- 2 cups chicken or vegetable broth
- 2 tablespoons olive oil
- Salt and pepper to taste
- Fresh cilantro or parsley, for garnish

Instructions:

1. In a large tagine or heavy-bottomed pot, heat the olive oil over medium heat. Add the lamb chunks and brown them on all sides. Remove the lamb from the pot and set aside.
2. In the same pot, add the chopped onion and minced garlic. Sauté until the onion becomes translucent and fragrant.
3. Add the ground cumin, coriander, cinnamon, paprika, ginger, and cayenne pepper (if using) to the pot. Stir well to coat the onions and garlic with the spices.
4. Return the browned lamb to the pot and mix it with the onion and spice mixture. Season with salt and pepper to taste.
5. Pour in the chicken or vegetable broth, ensuring that the lamb is fully submerged. Bring the mixture to a boil, then reduce the heat to low and cover the pot. Let the tagine simmer for 2 hours, or until the lamb is tender and easily pulls apart with a fork.

6. After 2 hours, add the dried apricots and whole almonds to the pot. Stir well to combine. Cover the pot again and let the tagine simmer for an additional 30 minutes, or until the apricots have plumped up and the almonds are tender.

7. Taste the tagine and adjust the seasoning if needed. If the sauce is too thin, you can simmer it uncovered for a few more minutes to thicken it slightly.

8. Serve the Lamb Tagine with Apricots and Almonds hot, garnished with fresh cilantro or parsley. It pairs well with couscous or warm crusty bread.

Nutrition information:
- Calories: 450
- Fat: 25g
- Carbohydrates: 25g
- Protein: 35g
- Fiber: 5g
- Sodium: 600mg

82. Grilled Salmon with Lemon Dill Sauce

Grilled Salmon with Lemon Dill Sauce is a delicious and healthy dish that is perfect for any occasion. The combination of the smoky grilled salmon and the tangy lemon dill sauce creates a burst of flavors that will leave your taste buds wanting more. This recipe is quick and easy to make, making it a great option for a weeknight dinner or a weekend barbecue.

Serving: 4 servings
Preparation time: 10 minutes
Ready time: 20 minutes

Ingredients:
- 4 salmon fillets (about 6 ounces each)
- Salt and pepper to taste
- 2 tablespoons olive oil
- 2 tablespoons fresh dill, chopped
- 2 tablespoons fresh lemon juice
- 1 tablespoon Dijon mustard

- 1 tablespoon honey
- 1 clove garlic, minced

Instructions:
1. Preheat your grill to medium-high heat.
2. Season the salmon fillets with salt and pepper on both sides.
3. In a small bowl, whisk together the olive oil, dill, lemon juice, Dijon mustard, honey, and minced garlic to make the lemon dill sauce.
4. Brush the grill grates with oil to prevent sticking.
5. Place the salmon fillets on the grill, skin side down, and cook for about 4-5 minutes per side, or until the salmon is cooked through and flakes easily with a fork.
6. During the last few minutes of grilling, brush the salmon fillets with the lemon dill sauce, reserving some for serving.
7. Remove the salmon from the grill and let it rest for a few minutes.
8. Serve the grilled salmon with the remaining lemon dill sauce on the side.

Nutrition information per Serving: - Calories: 350
- Fat: 20g
- Protein: 35g
- Carbohydrates: 6g
- Fiber: 1g
- Sugar: 4g
- Sodium: 300mg
Note: Nutrition information may vary depending on the size and type of salmon used.

83. Chicken Tikki Masala

Chicken Tikki Masala is a popular Indian dish that consists of tender chicken pieces cooked in a rich and flavorful tomato-based sauce. This dish is known for its aromatic spices and creamy texture, making it a favorite among many food enthusiasts. Whether you're a fan of Indian cuisine or looking to try something new, Chicken Tikki Masala is sure to satisfy your taste buds.
Serving:
This recipe serves 4 people.

Preparation time:
Preparation time for Chicken Tikki Masala is approximately 20 minutes.
Ready time:
The dish will be ready to serve in about 40 minutes.

Ingredients:
- 500 grams boneless chicken, cut into bite-sized pieces
- 1 cup plain yogurt
- 2 tablespoons vegetable oil
- 1 large onion, finely chopped
- 3 cloves of garlic, minced
- 1-inch piece of ginger, grated
- 2 teaspoons ground cumin
- 2 teaspoons ground coriander
- 1 teaspoon turmeric powder
- 1 teaspoon paprika
- 1 teaspoon garam masala
- 1 teaspoon salt (or to taste)
- 1 can (400 grams) diced tomatoes
- 1 cup heavy cream
- Fresh cilantro, chopped (for garnish)

Instructions:
1. In a bowl, marinate the chicken pieces with yogurt, ginger, garlic, cumin, coriander, turmeric, paprika, garam masala, and salt. Mix well and let it marinate for at least 30 minutes, or overnight in the refrigerator for more flavor.
2. Heat the vegetable oil in a large skillet or pan over medium heat. Add the chopped onion and sauté until it becomes translucent and lightly golden.
3. Add the marinated chicken to the pan and cook until it is browned on all sides, about 5-7 minutes.
4. Pour in the diced tomatoes and stir well. Reduce the heat to low, cover the pan, and let it simmer for about 15-20 minutes, or until the chicken is cooked through and tender.
5. Stir in the heavy cream and let it simmer for an additional 5 minutes, allowing the flavors to meld together.
6. Garnish with fresh cilantro and serve hot with steamed rice or naan bread.

Nutrition information:
- Calories: 350 per Serving: - Fat: 20g
- Carbohydrates: 10g
- Protein: 30g
- Fiber: 2g
- Sodium: 600mg

Note: The nutrition information provided is an estimate and may vary depending on the specific Ingredients used.

84. Irish Soda Farls

Irish Soda Farls are traditional Irish bread that are quick and easy to make. These delicious breads are made with simple Ingredients and have a unique texture and flavor. They are perfect for breakfast, brunch, or as a side dish for soups and stews.

Serving:
This recipe makes 4 farls.
Preparation time:
10 minutes
Ready time:
20 minutes

Ingredients:
- 2 cups all-purpose flour
- 1 teaspoon baking soda
- 1/2 teaspoon salt
- 1 cup buttermilk
- Butter or oil for cooking

Instructions:
1. In a large mixing bowl, whisk together the flour, baking soda, and salt.
2. Make a well in the center of the dry Ingredients and pour in the buttermilk.
3. Using a wooden spoon or your hands, mix the Ingredients together until a soft dough forms. If the dough is too sticky, add a little more flour.
4. Turn the dough out onto a lightly floured surface and knead it gently for a minute until it comes together.

5. Divide the dough into 4 equal portions and shape each portion into a round, flat farl about 1/2 inch thick.
6. Heat a griddle or a large frying pan over medium heat and lightly grease it with butter or oil.
7. Cook the farls for about 5-7 minutes on each side, or until they are golden brown and cooked through.
8. Remove the farls from the griddle and let them cool slightly before serving.

Nutrition information per Serving: - Calories: 200
- Fat: 2g
- Carbohydrates: 40g
- Protein: 6g
- Fiber: 2g
Note: Nutrition information may vary depending on the specific Ingredients and brands used.

85. Beef and Broccoli Stir-Fry

Beef and Broccoli Stir-Fry is a delicious and nutritious dish that combines tender beef, crisp broccoli, and a flavorful sauce. This quick and easy recipe is perfect for a weeknight dinner and will satisfy your cravings for Chinese takeout. With a few simple Ingredients and minimal preparation time, you can enjoy this homemade stir-fry in no time.
Serving: 4 servings
Preparation time: 15 minutes
Ready time: 25 minutes

Ingredients:
- 1 lb beef sirloin, thinly sliced
- 2 cups broccoli florets
- 1 tablespoon vegetable oil
- 3 cloves garlic, minced
- 1 teaspoon ginger, grated
- 1/4 cup soy sauce
- 2 tablespoons oyster sauce
- 1 tablespoon cornstarch
- 1/4 cup water

- 1 teaspoon sesame oil
- Salt and pepper to taste
- Cooked rice or noodles for Serving:

Instructions:
1. In a small bowl, whisk together soy sauce, oyster sauce, cornstarch, water, and sesame oil. Set aside.
2. Heat vegetable oil in a large skillet or wok over medium-high heat.
3. Add minced garlic and grated ginger to the skillet and sauté for about 1 minute until fragrant.
4. Add the sliced beef to the skillet and cook for 3-4 minutes until browned. Season with salt and pepper to taste.
5. Remove the beef from the skillet and set aside.
6. In the same skillet, add the broccoli florets and stir-fry for 2-3 minutes until they turn bright green and slightly tender.
7. Return the beef to the skillet and pour the sauce mixture over the beef and broccoli.
8. Stir-fry for an additional 2-3 minutes until the sauce thickens and coats the beef and broccoli evenly.
9. Remove from heat and serve the beef and broccoli stir-fry over cooked rice or noodles.

Nutrition information per Serving: - Calories: 320
- Fat: 12g
- Carbohydrates: 15g
- Protein: 35g
- Fiber: 3g
- Sugar: 4g
- Sodium: 900mg
Note: Nutrition information may vary depending on the specific Ingredients and brands used.

86. Shrimp Pad Thai

Shrimp Pad Thai is a popular Thai dish that combines stir-fried rice noodles with succulent shrimp, crunchy vegetables, and a tangy sauce. This flavorful and satisfying dish is perfect for a quick and easy weeknight dinner or for entertaining guests.

Serving: 4 servings
Preparation time: 15 minutes
Ready time: 25 minutes

Ingredients:
- 8 ounces rice noodles
- 1 pound shrimp, peeled and deveined
- 2 tablespoons vegetable oil
- 3 cloves garlic, minced
- 1 red bell pepper, thinly sliced
- 1 cup bean sprouts
- 2 green onions, sliced
- 2 eggs, lightly beaten
- 1/4 cup chopped peanuts
- Lime wedges, for Serving: For the sauce:
- 3 tablespoons fish sauce
- 2 tablespoons soy sauce
- 2 tablespoons tamarind paste
- 2 tablespoons brown sugar
- 1 tablespoon rice vinegar
- 1/2 teaspoon red pepper flakes (optional)

Instructions:
1. Cook the rice noodles according to package instructions. Drain and set aside.
2. In a small bowl, whisk together the fish sauce, soy sauce, tamarind paste, brown sugar, rice vinegar, and red pepper flakes (if using). Set aside.
3. Heat 1 tablespoon of vegetable oil in a large skillet or wok over medium-high heat. Add the shrimp and cook until pink and cooked through, about 2-3 minutes per side. Remove the shrimp from the skillet and set aside.
4. In the same skillet, add another tablespoon of vegetable oil. Add the minced garlic and cook for 1 minute until fragrant. Add the sliced bell pepper and cook for another 2 minutes until slightly softened.
5. Push the vegetables to one side of the skillet and pour the beaten eggs into the other side. Scramble the eggs until cooked through, then mix them with the vegetables.

6. Add the cooked rice noodles and the prepared sauce to the skillet. Toss everything together until well combined and heated through, about 2-3 minutes.

7. Add the cooked shrimp, bean sprouts, and sliced green onions to the skillet. Toss again to combine all the Ingredients.

8. Remove from heat and garnish with chopped peanuts. Serve hot with lime wedges on the side.

Nutrition information:
- Calories: 420
- Fat: 12g
- Carbohydrates: 55g
- Protein: 25g
- Fiber: 4g
- Sugar: 10g
- Sodium: 1200mg

87. Guinness Chocolate Cake

Indulge in the rich and decadent flavors of our Guinness Chocolate Cake. This moist and luscious dessert combines the deep flavors of Guinness stout with the sweetness of chocolate, creating a perfect balance of taste. Whether you're a fan of Guinness or simply love chocolate, this cake is sure to satisfy your cravings.

Serving: 12 servings
Preparation time: 20 minutes
Ready time: 1 hour 30 minutes

Ingredients:
- 1 cup Guinness stout
- 1 cup unsalted butter
- 3/4 cup unsweetened cocoa powder
- 2 cups all-purpose flour
- 2 cups granulated sugar
- 1 1/2 teaspoons baking soda
- 1/2 teaspoon salt
- 2 large eggs
- 2/3 cup sour cream

- 1 teaspoon vanilla extract

Instructions:
1. Preheat your oven to 350°F (175°C) and grease a 9-inch round cake pan.
2. In a small saucepan, heat the Guinness and butter over medium heat until the butter has melted. Remove from heat and whisk in the cocoa powder until smooth. Set aside to cool slightly.
3. In a large mixing bowl, combine the flour, sugar, baking soda, and salt.
4. In a separate bowl, beat the eggs, sour cream, and vanilla extract until well combined.
5. Gradually pour the Guinness mixture into the egg mixture, stirring constantly.
6. Slowly add the wet Ingredients to the dry Ingredients, mixing until just combined. Be careful not to overmix.
7. Pour the batter into the prepared cake pan and smooth the top with a spatula.
8. Bake for approximately 45-50 minutes, or until a toothpick inserted into the center comes out clean.
9. Remove the cake from the oven and let it cool in the pan for 10 minutes. Then, transfer it to a wire rack to cool completely.
10. Once the cake has cooled, you can frost it with your favorite chocolate frosting or dust it with powdered sugar.

Nutrition information per Serving: - Calories: 380
- Fat: 18g
- Carbohydrates: 52g
- Protein: 5g
- Fiber: 3g
- Sugar: 34g
- Sodium: 320mg
Note: Nutrition information may vary depending on the specific Ingredients and brands used.

88. Lamb Korma

Lamb Korma is a delicious and aromatic Indian dish that is perfect for those who enjoy the flavors of Indian cuisine. This rich and creamy curry is made with tender pieces of lamb cooked in a flavorful blend of spices and yogurt. It is a perfect dish to serve at dinner parties or to enjoy with your family on a cozy night in.

Serving: 4 servings
Preparation time: 15 minutes
Ready time: 1 hour 30 minutes

Ingredients:
- 1.5 pounds of boneless lamb, cut into bite-sized pieces
- 1 cup plain yogurt
- 2 tablespoons vegetable oil
- 2 medium onions, finely chopped
- 4 cloves of garlic, minced
- 1-inch piece of ginger, grated
- 2 teaspoons ground cumin
- 2 teaspoons ground coriander
- 1 teaspoon ground turmeric
- 1 teaspoon ground cardamom
- 1 teaspoon chili powder (adjust according to your spice preference)
- 1 cup tomato puree
- 1 cup water
- 1/2 cup heavy cream
- Salt, to taste
- Fresh cilantro, for garnish

Instructions:
1. In a large bowl, marinate the lamb pieces with yogurt, salt, and half of the minced garlic. Let it sit for at least 30 minutes or overnight in the refrigerator for better flavor absorption.
2. Heat the vegetable oil in a large, deep skillet or Dutch oven over medium heat. Add the chopped onions and sauté until they turn golden brown.
3. Add the remaining minced garlic and grated ginger to the skillet and cook for another minute until fragrant.
4. In a small bowl, mix together the ground cumin, coriander, turmeric, cardamom, and chili powder. Add this spice mixture to the skillet and cook for a minute, stirring constantly to prevent burning.
5. Add the marinated lamb pieces to the skillet and cook until they are browned on all sides.

6. Stir in the tomato puree and water, then reduce the heat to low. Cover the skillet and let the lamb simmer for about 1 hour or until it becomes tender and the flavors meld together.

7. Stir in the heavy cream and cook for an additional 5 minutes to thicken the sauce. Adjust the salt according to your taste.

8. Garnish with fresh cilantro and serve hot with steamed rice or naan bread.

Nutrition information:
- Calories: 450
- Fat: 30g
- Carbohydrates: 10g
- Protein: 35g
- Fiber: 2g
- Sodium: 400mg

Note: The nutrition information provided is an estimate and may vary depending on the specific Ingredients used.

89. Baked Stuffed Lobster

Baked Stuffed Lobster is a delicious and indulgent seafood dish that is perfect for special occasions or a fancy dinner at home. This recipe combines succulent lobster meat with a flavorful stuffing, creating a dish that is sure to impress your guests. With a crispy golden crust and a tender, juicy interior, this Baked Stuffed Lobster is a true showstopper.

Serving: 2 servings
Preparation time: 30 minutes
Ready time: 1 hour 30 minutes

Ingredients:
- 2 live lobsters (about 1 ½ pounds each)
- 1 cup fresh breadcrumbs
- 1/4 cup melted butter
- 1/4 cup finely chopped onion
- 1/4 cup finely chopped celery
- 1/4 cup finely chopped red bell pepper
- 2 cloves garlic, minced
- 1/4 cup chopped fresh parsley

- 1/4 teaspoon dried thyme
- 1/4 teaspoon dried oregano
- 1/4 teaspoon salt
- 1/4 teaspoon black pepper
- 1/4 cup grated Parmesan cheese
- Lemon wedges, for Serving:

Instructions:
1. Preheat your oven to 375°F (190°C).
2. Prepare the lobsters by placing them in the freezer for about 15 minutes. This will help sedate them before cooking.
3. In a large pot, bring water to a boil. Add the lobsters and cook for about 5 minutes. Remove them from the pot and let them cool slightly.
4. Once the lobsters are cool enough to handle, use a sharp knife to carefully split them in half lengthwise. Remove the green tomalley and rinse the lobsters under cold water to remove any remaining debris.
5. In a large bowl, combine the breadcrumbs, melted butter, onion, celery, red bell pepper, garlic, parsley, thyme, oregano, salt, black pepper, and Parmesan cheese. Mix well until all the Ingredients are evenly incorporated.
6. Place the lobster halves on a baking sheet, cut side up. Divide the breadcrumb mixture evenly among the lobster halves, pressing it gently into the cavities.
7. Bake the stuffed lobsters in the preheated oven for about 25-30 minutes, or until the stuffing is golden brown and the lobster meat is opaque and cooked through.
8. Remove the lobsters from the oven and let them cool for a few minutes before serving.
9. Serve the Baked Stuffed Lobster with lemon wedges on the side for squeezing over the lobster meat.

Nutrition information:
- Calories: 450
- Fat: 20g
- Carbohydrates: 20g
- Protein: 45g
- Fiber: 2g
- Sugar: 3g
- Sodium: 900mg

Note: Nutrition information may vary depending on the size of the lobsters used.

90. Chicken Marsala

Chicken Marsala is a classic Italian dish that features tender chicken breasts cooked in a rich and flavorful Marsala wine sauce. This dish is perfect for a special occasion or a cozy weeknight dinner. The combination of savory chicken, earthy mushrooms, and sweet Marsala wine creates a delicious and satisfying meal.
Serving: 4 servings
Preparation time: 10 minutes
Ready time: 30 minutes

Ingredients:
- 4 boneless, skinless chicken breasts
- Salt and pepper, to taste
- 1/2 cup all-purpose flour
- 4 tablespoons unsalted butter, divided
- 1 tablespoon olive oil
- 8 ounces mushrooms, sliced
- 2 cloves garlic, minced
- 1 cup Marsala wine
- 1 cup chicken broth
- 1/2 cup heavy cream
- Fresh parsley, chopped (for garnish)

Instructions:
1. Start by pounding the chicken breasts to an even thickness, about 1/2 inch. Season both sides with salt and pepper.
2. Place the flour in a shallow dish and dredge each chicken breast in the flour, shaking off any excess.
3. In a large skillet, melt 2 tablespoons of butter and olive oil over medium-high heat. Add the chicken breasts and cook for about 4-5 minutes per side, or until golden brown and cooked through. Remove the chicken from the skillet and set aside.

4. In the same skillet, melt the remaining 2 tablespoons of butter. Add the mushrooms and garlic, and cook until the mushrooms are tender and golden brown, about 5 minutes.

5. Pour in the Marsala wine and chicken broth, scraping the bottom of the skillet to release any browned bits. Bring the mixture to a simmer and cook for about 5 minutes, or until the liquid has reduced by half.

6. Stir in the heavy cream and return the chicken breasts to the skillet. Simmer for an additional 2-3 minutes, or until the sauce has thickened slightly and the chicken is heated through.

7. Serve the Chicken Marsala over cooked pasta or mashed potatoes. Garnish with fresh parsley.

Nutrition information per Serving: - Calories: 420
- Fat: 22g
- Carbohydrates: 16g
- Protein: 32g
- Fiber: 1g
- Sugar: 4g
- Sodium: 520mg

91. Irish Barmbrack

Irish Barmbrack is a traditional Irish fruitcake that is typically enjoyed during Halloween and other festive occasions. This delicious treat is packed with dried fruits and spices, making it a perfect accompaniment to a cup of tea or coffee. The name "Barmbrack" comes from the Irish word "bairín breac," which means "speckled loaf," referring to the fruit and peel that are scattered throughout the cake. Follow this recipe to create your own homemade Irish Barmbrack and indulge in a slice of Irish tradition.

Serving: 8-10 slices
Preparation time: 20 minutes
Ready time: 1 hour 30 minutes

Ingredients:
- 2 cups mixed dried fruits (such as raisins, currants, and sultanas)
- 1 cup strong black tea
- 1 cup all-purpose flour

- 1 teaspoon baking powder
- 1/2 teaspoon ground cinnamon
- 1/4 teaspoon ground nutmeg
- 1/4 teaspoon ground cloves
- 1/4 teaspoon salt
- 1/2 cup brown sugar
- 1 egg, beaten
- 1 tablespoon honey
- 1 tablespoon melted butter
- 1 tablespoon orange zest
- 1 tablespoon lemon zest

Instructions:
1. In a large bowl, combine the mixed dried fruits and black tea. Let them soak for at least 1 hour, or overnight if possible. This will plump up the fruits and infuse them with the tea flavor.
2. Preheat your oven to 350°F (175°C). Grease and line a 9-inch round cake pan with parchment paper.
3. In a separate bowl, whisk together the all-purpose flour, baking powder, ground cinnamon, ground nutmeg, ground cloves, and salt. Set aside.
4. Once the dried fruits have soaked, drain any excess liquid and reserve 1/4 cup of the soaking liquid.
5. In a large mixing bowl, combine the soaked fruits, brown sugar, beaten egg, honey, melted butter, orange zest, and lemon zest. Mix well until all the Ingredients are evenly incorporated.
6. Gradually add the dry Ingredient mixture to the fruit mixture, stirring until just combined. Be careful not to overmix.
7. Pour the batter into the prepared cake pan and smooth the top with a spatula.
8. Bake in the preheated oven for 1 hour, or until a toothpick inserted into the center comes out clean.
9. Remove the Barmbrack from the oven and let it cool in the pan for 10 minutes. Then, transfer it to a wire rack to cool completely.
10. Once cooled, slice the Barmbrack into 8-10 servings and enjoy!

Nutrition information per Serving: - Calories: 250
- Fat: 3g
- Carbohydrates: 55g
- Fiber: 3g

- Protein: 4g
- Sugar: 35g
- Sodium: 120mg
Note: Nutrition information may vary depending on the specific
Ingredients and brands used.

92. Beef and Vegetable Skewers

Beef and Vegetable Skewers are a delicious and healthy option for a
quick and easy meal. These skewers are packed with tender beef, colorful
vegetables, and flavorful seasonings. Whether you're grilling outdoors or
using an indoor grill pan, these skewers are sure to be a hit with family
and friends.
Serving: 4 servings
Preparation time: 20 minutes
Ready time: 30 minutes

Ingredients:
- 1 pound beef sirloin, cut into 1-inch cubes
- 1 red bell pepper, cut into 1-inch pieces
- 1 green bell pepper, cut into 1-inch pieces
- 1 yellow bell pepper, cut into 1-inch pieces
- 1 red onion, cut into 1-inch pieces
- 8 cherry tomatoes
- 2 tablespoons olive oil
- 2 tablespoons soy sauce
- 2 cloves garlic, minced
- 1 teaspoon dried oregano
- 1 teaspoon paprika
- Salt and pepper, to taste
- Wooden skewers, soaked in water for 30 minutes

Instructions:
1. In a large bowl, combine the olive oil, soy sauce, minced garlic, dried
oregano, paprika, salt, and pepper. Mix well to create a marinade.
2. Add the beef cubes to the marinade and toss to coat. Allow the beef to
marinate for at least 15 minutes, or up to overnight in the refrigerator.
3. Preheat your grill or grill pan over medium-high heat.

4. Thread the marinated beef, bell peppers, red onion, and cherry tomatoes onto the soaked wooden skewers, alternating between the Ingredients.

5. Place the skewers on the preheated grill and cook for about 10-12 minutes, turning occasionally, until the beef is cooked to your desired level of doneness and the vegetables are tender.

6. Remove the skewers from the grill and let them rest for a few minutes before serving.

7. Serve the beef and vegetable skewers hot with your favorite dipping sauce or alongside a fresh salad or rice.

Nutrition information per Serving: - Calories: 280
- Protein: 25g
- Fat: 15g
- Carbohydrates: 12g
- Fiber: 3g
- Sugar: 6g
- Sodium: 480mg

93. Cajun Shrimp and Sausage Jambalaya

Cajun Shrimp and Sausage Jambalaya is a flavorful and hearty dish that originates from the southern United States. This one-pot meal combines succulent shrimp, spicy sausage, and aromatic vegetables with a blend of Cajun spices and rice. It's a perfect dish to warm you up on a chilly evening or to serve at a gathering with friends and family.
Serving: 4 servings
Preparation time: 15 minutes
Ready time: 45 minutes

Ingredients:
- 1 pound large shrimp, peeled and deveined
- 1 pound smoked sausage, sliced into rounds
- 1 onion, diced
- 1 green bell pepper, diced
- 2 celery stalks, diced
- 3 cloves of garlic, minced
- 1 can (14.5 ounces) diced tomatoes

- 2 cups chicken broth
- 1 cup long-grain white rice
- 2 tablespoons Cajun seasoning
- 1 teaspoon dried thyme
- 1 teaspoon paprika
- 1/2 teaspoon cayenne pepper (adjust to taste)
- Salt and black pepper to taste
- 2 tablespoons vegetable oil
- Fresh parsley, chopped (for garnish)

Instructions:
1. In a large pot or Dutch oven, heat the vegetable oil over medium heat. Add the sausage slices and cook until browned, about 5 minutes. Remove the sausage from the pot and set aside.
2. In the same pot, add the onion, bell pepper, and celery. Sauté until the vegetables are softened, about 5 minutes. Add the minced garlic and cook for an additional minute.
3. Stir in the diced tomatoes (with their juice), chicken broth, rice, Cajun seasoning, dried thyme, paprika, cayenne pepper, salt, and black pepper. Bring the mixture to a boil.
4. Reduce the heat to low, cover the pot, and simmer for 20 minutes, or until the rice is cooked and most of the liquid is absorbed.
5. Meanwhile, season the shrimp with salt and black pepper. In a separate skillet, heat a tablespoon of vegetable oil over medium-high heat. Add the shrimp and cook until pink and opaque, about 2-3 minutes per side. Remove the shrimp from the skillet and set aside.
6. Once the rice is cooked, add the cooked sausage and shrimp to the pot. Stir gently to combine all the Ingredients. Cover the pot and let it sit for 5 minutes to allow the flavors to meld together.
7. Serve the Cajun Shrimp and Sausage Jambalaya hot, garnished with fresh parsley.

Nutrition information (per serving):
- Calories: 480
- Fat: 24g
- Carbohydrates: 35g
- Protein: 32g
- Fiber: 3g
- Sugar: 4g
- Sodium: 1200mg

94. Irish Stout Beef Stew

Irish Stout Beef Stew is a hearty and flavorful dish that combines tender beef, vegetables, and the rich taste of stout beer. This traditional Irish recipe is perfect for cold winter nights or St. Patrick's Day celebrations. The slow cooking process allows the flavors to meld together, resulting in a comforting and satisfying meal.

Serving: 4-6 servings
Preparation time: 20 minutes
Ready time: 2 hours 30 minutes

Ingredients:
- 2 pounds beef stew meat, cut into bite-sized pieces
- 2 tablespoons vegetable oil
- 1 large onion, diced
- 3 cloves garlic, minced
- 4 carrots, peeled and sliced
- 2 celery stalks, sliced
- 1 pound potatoes, peeled and cubed
- 2 tablespoons tomato paste
- 2 cups beef broth
- 1 cup Irish stout beer (such as Guinness)
- 2 bay leaves
- 1 teaspoon dried thyme
- Salt and pepper, to taste
- Chopped fresh parsley, for garnish (optional)

Instructions:
1. In a large pot or Dutch oven, heat the vegetable oil over medium-high heat. Add the beef stew meat and cook until browned on all sides. Remove the meat from the pot and set aside.
2. In the same pot, add the diced onion and minced garlic. Sauté until the onion becomes translucent and fragrant, about 5 minutes.
3. Add the carrots, celery, and potatoes to the pot. Stir in the tomato paste and cook for an additional 2 minutes.

4. Return the browned beef stew meat to the pot. Pour in the beef broth and Irish stout beer. Add the bay leaves and dried thyme. Season with salt and pepper to taste.

5. Bring the stew to a boil, then reduce the heat to low. Cover the pot and simmer for 2 hours, or until the beef is tender and the flavors have melded together.

6. Remove the bay leaves from the stew before serving. Garnish with chopped fresh parsley, if desired.

Nutrition information:
- Calories: 350 per Serving: - Fat: 12g
- Carbohydrates: 25g
- Protein: 30g
- Fiber: 4g
- Sodium: 600mg
Note: Nutrition information may vary depending on the specific Ingredients and brands used.

95. Chicken Fettuccine Alfredo

Chicken Fettuccine Alfredo is a classic Italian dish that combines tender chicken, creamy Alfredo sauce, and perfectly cooked fettuccine pasta. This rich and indulgent meal is perfect for a special occasion or a comforting weeknight dinner. With just a few simple Ingredients and easy steps, you can create a restaurant-quality dish right in your own kitchen.

Serving: 4 servings
Preparation time: 10 minutes
Ready time: 30 minutes

Ingredients:
- 8 ounces fettuccine pasta
- 2 boneless, skinless chicken breasts
- Salt and pepper, to taste
- 2 tablespoons olive oil
- 4 cloves garlic, minced
- 1 cup heavy cream
- 1 cup grated Parmesan cheese

- 1/2 cup unsalted butter
- Fresh parsley, chopped (for garnish)

Instructions:
1. Cook the fettuccine pasta according to the package instructions until al dente. Drain and set aside.
2. Season the chicken breasts with salt and pepper on both sides. In a large skillet, heat the olive oil over medium-high heat. Add the chicken breasts and cook for about 6-8 minutes per side, or until cooked through and no longer pink in the center. Remove the chicken from the skillet and let it rest for a few minutes before slicing it into thin strips.
3. In the same skillet, add the minced garlic and cook for about 1 minute, until fragrant. Reduce the heat to low and add the heavy cream, Parmesan cheese, and butter. Stir continuously until the sauce is smooth and creamy.
4. Add the cooked fettuccine pasta to the skillet with the sauce and toss until the pasta is well coated. Cook for an additional 2-3 minutes, until the pasta is heated through.
5. Serve the Chicken Fettuccine Alfredo in individual plates or bowls. Top with the sliced chicken and garnish with fresh parsley.
6. Enjoy your homemade Chicken Fettuccine Alfredo!

Nutrition information:
- Calories: 750
- Fat: 48g
- Carbohydrates: 50g
- Protein: 35g
- Fiber: 2g

96. Smoked Salmon and Cream Cheese Dip

This Smoked Salmon and Cream Cheese Dip is a delightful and creamy appetizer that is perfect for any occasion. The combination of smoky salmon and smooth cream cheese creates a rich and flavorful dip that will leave your guests wanting more. Whether you're hosting a party or simply looking for a delicious snack, this recipe is sure to impress.
Serving:
This recipe serves approximately 6-8 people.

Preparation time:
Preparation time for this dip is approximately 10 minutes.
Ready time:
The dip will be ready to serve immediately after preparation.

Ingredients:
- 8 ounces of smoked salmon, finely chopped
- 8 ounces of cream cheese, softened
- 1/4 cup of sour cream
- 2 tablespoons of fresh dill, chopped
- 1 tablespoon of lemon juice
- 1/2 teaspoon of garlic powder
- Salt and pepper to taste
- Crackers or sliced baguette, for Serving:

Instructions:
1. In a medium-sized bowl, combine the softened cream cheese, sour cream, fresh dill, lemon juice, garlic powder, salt, and pepper. Mix well until all the Ingredients are fully incorporated.
2. Gently fold in the finely chopped smoked salmon, making sure it is evenly distributed throughout the dip.
3. Taste the dip and adjust the seasoning if needed, adding more salt, pepper, or lemon juice according to your preference.
4. Transfer the dip to a serving bowl and garnish with a sprig of fresh dill.
5. Serve the Smoked Salmon and Cream Cheese Dip with your choice of crackers or sliced baguette.

Nutrition information:
- Serving size: 2 tablespoons
- Calories: 90
- Total fat: 7g
- Saturated fat: 4g
- Cholesterol: 25mg
- Sodium: 180mg
- Total carbohydrates: 2g
- Protein: 5g
Note: Nutrition information may vary depending on the specific brands and quantities of Ingredients used.

97. Irish Coffee Mousse

Irish Coffee Mousse is a delightful dessert that combines the rich flavors of coffee and Irish whiskey with a light and creamy mousse. This indulgent treat is perfect for coffee lovers and those who enjoy a touch of Irish spirit in their desserts. With its smooth texture and irresistible taste, this Irish Coffee Mousse is sure to impress your guests or satisfy your sweet tooth.

Serving: 4 servings
Preparation time: 20 minutes
Ready time: 4 hours (including chilling time)

Ingredients:
- 2 tablespoons instant coffee granules
- 2 tablespoons hot water
- 2 tablespoons Irish whiskey
- 1 cup heavy cream
- 1/4 cup powdered sugar
- 1 teaspoon vanilla extract
- 2 egg yolks
- 2 tablespoons granulated sugar
- 1/4 cup boiling water
- 1 teaspoon gelatin powder
- Whipped cream and chocolate shavings, for garnish (optional)

Instructions:
1. In a small bowl, dissolve the instant coffee granules in hot water. Stir in the Irish whiskey and set aside to cool.
2. In a mixing bowl, whip the heavy cream, powdered sugar, and vanilla extract until soft peaks form. Set aside.
3. In a separate bowl, whisk together the egg yolks and granulated sugar until pale and creamy.
4. In a small saucepan, bring the boiling water to a simmer. Sprinkle the gelatin powder over the simmering water and whisk until completely dissolved.
5. Slowly pour the dissolved gelatin mixture into the egg yolk mixture, whisking constantly to prevent curdling.

6. Gradually add the coffee and whiskey mixture to the egg yolk mixture, whisking continuously.

7. Gently fold the whipped cream into the coffee and whiskey mixture until well combined.

8. Divide the mousse mixture among serving glasses or bowls. Cover and refrigerate for at least 4 hours, or until set.

9. Before serving, garnish with a dollop of whipped cream and a sprinkle of chocolate shavings, if desired.

Nutrition information per Serving: - Calories: 280
- Fat: 20g
- Carbohydrates: 15g
- Protein: 2g
- Sugar: 12g
- Sodium: 20mg

Note: The nutrition information provided is an estimate and may vary depending on the specific Ingredients used.

98. Beef Bulgogi

Beef Bulgogi is a popular Korean dish that features thinly sliced beef marinated in a flavorful sauce and then grilled or stir-fried. This dish is known for its tender and juicy meat, combined with the perfect balance of sweet and savory flavors. It is often served with steamed rice and a variety of side dishes, making it a complete and satisfying meal.

Serving: 4 servings
Preparation time: 15 minutes
Ready time: 1 hour 15 minutes

Ingredients:
- 1 pound beef sirloin, thinly sliced
- 1/4 cup soy sauce
- 2 tablespoons brown sugar
- 2 tablespoons sesame oil
- 2 tablespoons rice wine or mirin
- 3 cloves garlic, minced
- 1 teaspoon grated ginger
- 1 tablespoon sesame seeds

- 2 green onions, thinly sliced
- 1 tablespoon vegetable oil
- Optional: sliced mushrooms, bell peppers, or onions for added flavor and texture

Instructions:

1. In a bowl, combine soy sauce, brown sugar, sesame oil, rice wine or mirin, minced garlic, grated ginger, sesame seeds, and green onions. Mix well to create the marinade.
2. Add the thinly sliced beef to the marinade and toss until all the meat is coated. Allow the beef to marinate for at least 1 hour in the refrigerator, or overnight for maximum flavor.
3. Heat a large skillet or grill pan over medium-high heat and add vegetable oil.
4. Once the oil is hot, add the marinated beef to the pan, reserving any excess marinade for later use.
5. Cook the beef for about 2-3 minutes per side, or until it is cooked to your desired level of doneness. If using additional vegetables, add them to the pan and cook until they are tender.
6. Pour the reserved marinade over the cooked beef and vegetables, stirring to combine. Cook for an additional 1-2 minutes to allow the flavors to meld together.
7. Remove the beef bulgogi from the heat and serve hot with steamed rice and your choice of side dishes.

Nutrition information per Serving: - Calories: 320
- Fat: 18g
- Carbohydrates: 9g
- Protein: 30g
- Fiber: 1g
- Sugar: 6g
- Sodium: 900mg
Note: Nutrition information may vary depending on the specific Ingredients and brands used.

99. Grilled Shrimp Tacos with Slaw

Grilled Shrimp Tacos with Slaw are a delicious and refreshing dish that combines the smoky flavors of grilled shrimp with a tangy slaw. These tacos are perfect for a summer barbecue or a quick and easy weeknight dinner. The combination of the juicy shrimp, crunchy slaw, and warm tortillas will leave you craving for more!

Serving: 4 servings

Preparation time: 20 minutes

Ready time: 30 minutes

Ingredients:
- 1 pound of large shrimp, peeled and deveined
- 2 tablespoons of olive oil
- 1 teaspoon of chili powder
- 1 teaspoon of garlic powder
- 1 teaspoon of paprika
- Salt and pepper to taste
- 8 small flour tortillas
- 1 cup of shredded cabbage
- 1/2 cup of shredded carrots
- 1/4 cup of chopped fresh cilantro
- 1/4 cup of mayonnaise
- 2 tablespoons of lime juice
- 1 tablespoon of honey
- Optional toppings: sliced avocado, diced tomatoes, chopped jalapenos

Instructions:
1. Preheat your grill to medium-high heat.
2. In a bowl, combine the olive oil, chili powder, garlic powder, paprika, salt, and pepper. Add the shrimp to the bowl and toss until they are evenly coated with the spice mixture.
3. Thread the shrimp onto skewers, making sure to leave a little space between each shrimp.
4. Place the shrimp skewers on the preheated grill and cook for 2-3 minutes per side, or until they are pink and opaque.
5. While the shrimp are grilling, prepare the slaw. In a separate bowl, combine the shredded cabbage, shredded carrots, chopped cilantro, mayonnaise, lime juice, and honey. Mix well until all the Ingredients are evenly combined.
6. Warm the flour tortillas on the grill for about 30 seconds per side, or until they are soft and pliable.

7. To assemble the tacos, spread a spoonful of the slaw onto each tortilla. Top with a few grilled shrimp and any optional toppings you desire.
8. Serve the Grilled Shrimp Tacos with Slaw immediately and enjoy!

Nutrition information:
- Calories: 350
- Fat: 15g
- Carbohydrates: 35g
- Protein: 20g
- Fiber: 4g

100. Chicken Souvlaki with Tzatziki Sauce

Chicken Souvlaki with Tzatziki Sauce is a delicious Greek dish that combines marinated chicken skewers with a creamy and refreshing tzatziki sauce. This flavorful and easy-to-make meal is perfect for a quick weeknight dinner or a weekend barbecue. The combination of tender chicken and tangy tzatziki sauce will transport your taste buds straight to the Mediterranean.
Serving: 4 servings
Preparation time: 15 minutes
Ready time: 30 minutes

Ingredients:
- 1.5 lbs boneless, skinless chicken breasts, cut into bite-sized pieces
- 1/4 cup olive oil
- 2 tablespoons lemon juice
- 2 cloves garlic, minced
- 1 teaspoon dried oregano
- 1/2 teaspoon salt
- 1/4 teaspoon black pepper
- 4 pita breads
- 1 cup cherry tomatoes, halved
- 1/2 red onion, thinly sliced
- Fresh parsley, chopped (for garnish)
For the Tzatziki Sauce:
- 1 cup Greek yogurt
- 1/2 cucumber, grated and squeezed to remove excess moisture

- 1 clove garlic, minced
- 1 tablespoon lemon juice
- 1 tablespoon fresh dill, chopped
- Salt and pepper to taste

Instructions:
1. In a bowl, combine the olive oil, lemon juice, minced garlic, dried oregano, salt, and black pepper. Mix well to create the marinade.
2. Add the chicken pieces to the marinade and toss until they are well coated. Allow the chicken to marinate for at least 15 minutes, or up to overnight in the refrigerator.
3. While the chicken is marinating, prepare the tzatziki sauce. In a separate bowl, combine the Greek yogurt, grated cucumber, minced garlic, lemon juice, fresh dill, salt, and pepper. Stir well to combine. Refrigerate until ready to serve.
4. Preheat your grill or grill pan over medium-high heat. Thread the marinated chicken pieces onto skewers.
5. Grill the chicken skewers for about 10-12 minutes, turning occasionally, until they are cooked through and slightly charred.
6. While the chicken is grilling, warm the pita breads on the grill for a minute on each side.
7. To serve, spread a generous amount of tzatziki sauce onto each warmed pita bread. Top with grilled chicken skewers, cherry tomatoes, sliced red onion, and a sprinkle of fresh parsley.
8. Serve the Chicken Souvlaki with Tzatziki Sauce immediately and enjoy!

Nutrition information:
- Calories: 380
- Fat: 12g
- Carbohydrates: 32g
- Protein: 36g
- Fiber: 3g

101. Irish Cola Ham

Irish Cola Ham is a delicious and flavorful dish that combines the sweetness of cola with the savory taste of ham. This traditional Irish recipe is perfect for special occasions or a hearty family meal. The ham is slow-cooked to perfection, resulting in tender and juicy meat that is sure to impress your guests. Serve it with your favorite sides for a complete and satisfying meal.

Serving: 8-10 servings
Preparation time: 15 minutes
Ready time: 3 hours 30 minutes

Ingredients:
- 1 (5-6 pounds) bone-in ham
- 2 cups cola
- 1 cup brown sugar
- 1 tablespoon whole cloves
- 1 tablespoon mustard powder
- 1 tablespoon ground black pepper

Instructions:
1. Preheat your oven to 325°F (165°C).
2. Place the ham in a large roasting pan, fat side up.
3. Score the fat in a diamond pattern, being careful not to cut too deep into the meat.
4. In a small saucepan, combine the cola, brown sugar, cloves, mustard powder, and black pepper. Bring the mixture to a boil over medium heat, stirring occasionally until the sugar has dissolved.
5. Pour the cola mixture over the ham, making sure to coat it evenly.
6. Cover the roasting pan tightly with aluminum foil.
7. Place the ham in the preheated oven and bake for 3 hours, or until the internal temperature reaches 140°F (60°C).
8. Every 30 minutes, baste the ham with the pan juices to keep it moist and flavorful.
9. Remove the foil during the last 30 minutes of cooking to allow the ham to brown.
10. Once cooked, remove the ham from the oven and let it rest for 10-15 minutes before slicing.
11. Serve the Irish Cola Ham warm with your favorite sides, such as mashed potatoes, roasted vegetables, or a fresh salad.

Nutrition information per Serving: - Calories: 350
- Total Fat: 12g
- Saturated Fat: 4g
- Cholesterol: 100mg

- Sodium: 1500mg
- Total Carbohydrate: 20g
- Dietary Fiber: 0g
- Sugars: 19g
- Protein: 40g

Note: Nutrition information may vary depending on the specific Ingredients and brands used.

CONCLUSION

"Ballymaloe Celebration: 101 Recipes for Special Occasions"

The cookbook "Ballymaloe Celebration: 101 Recipes for Special Occasions" is a perfect choice for any special occasion feast. Offering a variety of flavors, techniques, and courses ranging from appetizers to dessert. Each recipe is made with only the finest, high quality seasonal ingredients, always offering fresh, vibrant flavors with simple steps for preparation. Whether you're serving a dinner party or hosting an outdoor event, this cookbook has a recipe to fit your every need.

From crispy fried Ballycotton battered monkfish to a sticky chicken marinated in bacon fat, each recipe is sure to impress even the most discerning guests. Traditional dishes like cottage pie, steak and Guinness Stew, and rhubarb crumble provide great comfort food, while modern takes on classic recipes such as smoked salmon and cream cheese sandwich cones and panna cota make for unique contributions to the meal. Not to mention the delicious and diverse selection of desserts, like miso ice cream and turmeric velvet cakes.

What makes Ballymaloe Celebrationtruly special is the ability to tailor the menu to your own tastes and what you'd like to provide for your guests—from a full-blown nine-course meal to a simple four-course special occasion dinner. With quick and easy instructions, even the most inexperienced of cooks can follow along with ease. The ingredients are always fresh and high-quality, offering an authentic Irish culinary experience.

The cookbook "Ballymaloe Celebration: 101 Recipes for Special Occasions" is the perfect guide for any festive gathering. It is filled with mouth-watering recipes that cater to all sorts of diets and occasions. This book will satisfy even the most ambitious cook. Through these easy-to-follow recipes, anyone can enjoy the traditional flavors of Ireland without breaking the bank or straining themselves. Whether you're celebrating a birthday, anniversary, or any other special event, these recipes will surely make it memorable. The delicious Irish cuisine and gourmet cooking instructions are sure to delight any guest. So break out the cookbook and start celebrating!

Printed in Great Britain
by Amazon

35049717R00086